Praise for *Exodus Preaching*

"The detailed sermon crafting strategies in *Exodus Preaching* are essential to the teaching and practice of transformative preaching. Gilbert's careful analysis of varied sermonic content and contexts reveals new and more viable forms of justice- and hope-filled proclamation. *Exodus Preaching* is an essential resource for anyone seeking to faithfully raise a prophetic voice in times like these."
—Teresa L. Fry Brown, Bandy Professor of Preaching, Candler School of Theology, Emory University, Atlanta, GA

"I am completely and utterly impressed with the scholarship of Kenyatta Gilbert. *Exodus Preaching* meets and exceeds the high bar established by his previous books. He is the preeminent homiletical mind and voice of a generation, and must be read and heard by anyone who values and regards high-quality preaching."
—Frank A. Thomas, Director of PhD Program in African American Preaching and Sacred Rhetoric, Christian Theological Seminary, Indianapolis, IN

"Kenyatta Gilbert's insightful and inclusive text speaks to those who preach and minister across multiple platforms. *Exodus Preaching* offers critical hermeneutic and homiletical methods and strategies for poetic and prophetic investigation. Furthermore, the text provides practical tools for a conscious construction of sermons that address the existential crisis faced by many while at the same time offering hope that reflects God's desire for human flourishing."
—Danielle Ayers, Minister of Social Justice, and Damien Durr, Executive Pastor/Community Development, Friendship-West Baptist Church, Dallas, TX

"Kenyatta Gilbert invites any preacher seeking to have integrity to the justice witness of scripture, to meet him in the most rewarding and challenging boot camp for thinking 'all things sermon'—particularly when faithfulness to the prophetic tradition is the pursuit. If spirituality is a lifetime of conversions, I have been *again* converted!"
—William H. Curtis, Senior Pastor, Mount Ararat Baptist Church, Pittsburgh, PA

KENYATTA R. GILBERT

EXODUS PREACHING

CRAFTING SERMONS ABOUT JUSTICE AND HOPE

Abingdon Press™

Nashville

EXODUS PREACHING:
CRAFTING SERMONS ABOUT JUSTICE AND HOPE

Copyright © 2018 by Kenyatta R. Gilbert

All rights reserved.

This book is printed on acid-free paper.

Library of Congress Cataloging-in-Publication Data has been requested.

ISBN: 978-1-5018-3257-4

Scripture quotations unless noted otherwise are taken from the New Revised Standard Version Bible, copyright © 1989 National Council of the Churches of Christ in the United States of America. Used by permission. All rights reserved worldwide. http://nrsvbibles.org/

Scripture quotations marked KJV are taken from The Authorized (King James) Version. Rights in the Authorized Version in the United Kingdom are vested in the Crown. Reproduced by permission of the Crown's patentee, Cambridge University Press.

18 19 20 21 22 23 24 25 26 27—10 9 8 7 6 5 4 3 2 1

MANUFACTURED IN THE UNITED STATES OF AMERICA

To the memory of
Professor Dale P. Andrews

Martin L. King Jr. Professor of Homiletics and Pastoral Theology,
Boston University 2005–2010

Cornelius Vanderbilt Chair and Distinguished Professor of Homiletics, Social Justice,
and Practical Theology,
Vanderbilt University Divinity School 2011–2017

Mentor, Colleague, and Prophetic Sage

CONTENTS

INTRODUCTION

A prophet not only speaks to a congregation, a prophet speaks to a generation.

—Delvin Atchison[1]

Times are dark. But hope remains in reach. Among the many words that leave the preacher's lips, no Christian preacher escapes the obligation to set this declaration before the people. Why? Because preaching is what *hope* looks like in our age of compassion fatigue, conspicuous consumption, and deadly violence. Though not an end in itself, preaching is a means by which God reminds a society of God's concern for community wellness, life, human dignity, and freedom in a less-than-perfect world. This is why preaching and preachers matter.

WHAT IS EXODUS PREACHING?

African American prophetic preaching (alternatively termed *Exodus preaching*) is "interpretation" that brings clarity to the sacred (the realities of God, revealed truth, highest moral values, and so on) and articulates what should be appropriate human response to the sacred. The preacher who preaches prophetically does not treat social justice (or other sacred values) as something independent from God but as being rooted in and emanating from God. *Exodus preaching* does not take place in a vacuum, nor is it self-generated discourse; rather, it is daring speech that offers a vision of divine intent. It reveals a picture of what God intends and expects of God's human creation—a

---

1. Quotation taken from Delvin Atchison's sermon "A Plea for the Prophetic," Ezekiel 37:1-14, delivered on June 15, 2014, in Houston, Texas, at the Mount Sinai Baptist Church.

picture that enables persons and faith communities to interpret their situation in light of God's justice, and to name as sin activities that frustrate God's life-giving purposes.

African American prophetic preaching is meditational speech. It bears no fundamental distinction from prophetic preaching in general, except to the extent that it is seen as God-summoned speech clothed in cultural particularity.[2] Contextual awareness in preaching helps us to see that we bring ourselves to the scriptural texts we interpret, and our seeing, if we see anything at all, is revealed through the lens of our lived experience. Regarding context and culture, one must keep in mind that Jesus of Nazareth was not a rich Palestinian Jew—though a revolutionary figure nonetheless—who lived more than two thousand years ago in a living community. In other words, Jesus had a specific ethnic and religious identity, and this is not insignificant given Western culture's enduring fascination and general depiction of Jesus as a Nordic martyr. A Jesus separated from his Judaic heritage and social location renders Jesus ahistorical, mythical, and incapable of saving humanity.

Because human beings are thrown into traditions and communities from which they take their personhood and socializations, racially and ethnically blind preaching can only exist in the colonized mind. This is fact, not fiction. As God-summoned proclamation that lifts and values the reality that sociocultural context shapes preachers and their sermons, *Exodus preaching* sees the homiletical life through the religious practices and lived experiences of Gentile Christians of African descent in North America and is written from this perspective.

THE EXODUS NARRATIVE

The Exodus story supplies preachers the most lyrically potent ground of sacredness for proclaiming hope in the face of human tragedy and collective suffering. The saints of old intoned sacred songs of suffering and deliverance such as "Go Down Moses, Down in Egyptland . . . tell ole' Pharaoh to let my people go" in their wearied throats as a tool of hope in the antebellum South. And with pen and voice, from the celebrated Black poet and abolitionist Phyllis Wheatley's "Letter to Reverend Samson Occum" (1774) to Martin L. King Jr.'s vision of a beloved community, for more than 240 years,

---

2. Kenyatta R. Gilbert, *A Pursued Justice: Black Preaching from the Great Migration to Civil Rights* (Waco, TX: Baylor University Press, 2016), 6.

the development of faith identity in Black churches has traditionally invested symbolic significance in the Exodus narrative.[3] But the Exodus story does not stand alone in the religious imaginations of African American Christians. Also linked to the Black Christian's spiritual quest is a persistent engagement with the prophetic literature and regard for the messianic witness of Jesus Christ. Historically, there have been no stronger biblical touchstones from which African American ministers have defined and refined their prophetic voices.

THE JOSHUA GENERATION

Exodus Preaching's primary aim is to advance practical strategies for preaching with a prophetic consciousness. Some strategies stem from dialogue I've had with students in my prophetic preaching course; others emanate from fireside chats with many of the young and mid-career clergy leaders whom I've been privileged to journey alongside as friend, colleague, and participant-observer. Others were fashioned from hearing and analyzing sermons from pioneering preachers such as J. Alfred Smith Sr., Jeremiah A. Wright Jr., James A. Forbes Jr., Katie Cannon, Brian K. Blount, and still others from my vocational corpus as teacher and preacher.

A new generation of African American preachers has emerged, speaking their wisdom throughout these pages, making important strides to overcome the blighting of hope in Black churches and communities today. To name a few, Ray Owens, Leslie Callahan, and Raphael Warnock lead congregations in Tulsa, Philadelphia, and Atlanta, respectively, and have earned PhDs in the areas of Christian social ethics, religion, and theology. Bold and thoughtful sermons reveal their prophetic consciousness. American religion historian Adam L. Bond's theo-biographic book recalls the prophetic wisdom of the late Samuel D. Proctor, one of America's most influential Black public theologians of the mid-to-late twentieth century.[4] Patrick Clayborn's doctoral

---

3. Rhonda Robinson Thomas, *Claiming Exodus: A Cultural History of Afro-Atlantic Identity, 1774–1903* (Waco, TX: Baylor University Press, 2013), 5.

4. See my book review of "The Imposing Preacher: Samuel DeWitt Proctor and Black Public Faith," *Homiletic*, vol. 39, no. 2 (2014). Closing the academy/church gap, akin to Proctor, Bond integrates professorial, administrative, and clerical roles as researcher, director of Virginia Union's Proctor School of Theology's Center for Lifelong Learning, and pastor of Providence Baptist Church in Ashland, Virginia, preparing future church leaders for prophetic ministry in both urban and rural contexts in the South.

dissertation situates the theologian and mystic Howard Thurman's preaching within the prophetic Black rhetorical tradition. Clayborn awakens the field to a reconsideration of Thurman's homiletical skill and poetic vision relative to his uncommon commitment to bridge the racial divide. Unharnessed by exacting religio-cultural constrictions present in local churches, homiletics scholar Luke Powery and social ethicist Jonathan Walton lead predominantly White-university chapel congregations, respectively, Duke University Chapel and Harvard Memorial Church. They practice ministry with an ecumenical embrace of persons and live into Thurman and King's poetic and inclusive vision of genuine fellowship. Alert to the challenges of shaping pedagogies for globally conscious preaching, homiletics professors Debra Mumford at Louisville Seminary, Union Theological Seminary, New York's Lisa Thompson, Yale Divinity's Donyelle McCray, Wesley Seminary's Veronice Miles, and Memphis Seminary's megachurch critic Paula McGee train the next generation of seminarians as the first African American women in their faculty roles. Bi-vocational scholar Wayne E. Croft Sr. occupies the Jeremiah A. Wright Sr. Homiletics chair at Lutheran Seminary in Philadelphia. Croft, a graduate of Drew Seminary's homiletics and liturgics program, balances classroom instruction with a full-time pastorate in West Chester, Pennsylvania.

Candace Simpson and Eboni Marshall Turman have preached from historic urban pulpits in New York City—churches with longstanding commitments to the work of social justice and community renewal. They proclaim the justice of God in spoken Word and seek to call their listeners to pragmatic tasks in the village. Trumpeting prophetic alarm to the myriad ongoing crises affecting Black life in inner-city Chicago, Otis Moss III, son of civil rights legend Otis Moss Jr. and successor to Jeremiah Wright Jr. at Trinity UCC, reaches both iPod and walkie-talkie generations with his poetic, lyrically deft hip-hop–injected sermons.

Princeton Seminary alumni Quincy Taft Heatley, Kirby Spivey Sr., and Bankole Akinbinu bring prophetic fire to their pulpits in Alexandria, Virginia; Nova Scotia, Canada; and Raleigh, North Carolina. The strident voice of Princeton alum Toby Sanders is one seldom noticed and appreciated. Sanders pastors the Beloved Community Church in Trenton, New Jersey, where his preaching seeks alignment with the teachings of Jesus in the spirit of Martin L. King's love ethic. Another example of a ministry tying together criticism and hope is Olu Brown's team-led Impact Church, one of the fastest-growing churches in Greater Atlanta. Impact prides itself on, as its motto states, "doing church differently." Using a conversational-style preaching approach, a shift from traditional modes that color much of African American preaching, Brown is intentional about fashioning his own rhetorical strategy to build and sustain a multiethnic, multiracial fellowship. Emory University professor of pastoral care and theology Gregory C. Ellison II claims the status of itinerant preacher. Ellison takes unconventional approaches in the sermon event. With baseball hat to the back, wireless spectacles, Nike sneakers, and a sport coat, Ellison channels the theological mystics and ties homiletical wit to prophetic witness in his passionate quest to call attention to the plight of young Black boys, which he describes as society's "muted and invisible" ones. Dante Quick's dynamic preaching in the once economically vibrant California port city of Vallejo—a city that filed for bankruptcy in 2008—provides an important West Coast example of how prophetic proclamation works toward emancipatory ends through community advocacy, establishing debt elimination counseling, and financial literacy seminars for his membership.

The creative shaping of Lora Hargrove's prophetic sermons in her DC-area suburban context proves instructive for emerging mid-career clerics, specifically for women who have apprenticed themselves to male or female senior ministers. From Sunday to Sunday Hargrove discerningly negotiates how she will speak to the pressing issues of the day from within the limits of an assistant pastor role. From early fascination with the preaching life of Martin Luther King Jr. to his current charge, Central Texas pastor Kerry Burkley Sr. connects orthodoxy (right belief) to orthopraxis (right practice) in spoken word each Sunday before his small Black Baptist congregation in Waco, Texas. Skillfully transcending ecclesial and mono-racial communal constraints, turning lectern into pulpit, he mentors and prepares Baylor University students for active engagement in community development.

Howard University School of Divinity alumni Cecil Duffie and Erica Williams, respectively serving as associate dean at the historic Andrew Rankin Memorial Chapel in Washington, DC, and field coordinator for the Moral Mondays Movement, represent a growing vanguard establishing their prophetic witness beyond the homiletics classroom at Howard. HUSD alumnus and Baltimore's Greater Paradise Christian Center "generation Y" youth pastor Brandon Harris, who serves as a ministry associate, possesses a fertile homiletical mind. A nimble wordsmith and classically trained musician, Harris yokes prophetic discourse to the Pentecostal fervor of his Apostolic Church tradition. His use of technology, social networking platforms, and ability to voice clarion calls as social-poet to Black millennials inspires hope in the segregated and economically blighted city. Despite his growing ministry profile in the trail of an inflamed city overrun with rioting after the tragic death of twenty-five-year-old Black male Freddie Gray, who died of injuries sustained while in police custody, Harris has firmly embraced his prophetic assignment while resisting the temptation toward political self-aggrandizement.

Liberty Hill Baptist Church of Cleveland pastor and community leader Mark L. Johnson Sr. serves as his congregation's priest, but has assumed a more visible public role as priest-prophet in the wake of the shooting death of Cleveland twelve-year-old Tamir Rice and amid the mass protests consequent to the acquittal of thirty-one-year-old White police officer Michael Brelo, who in 2012, following what police and witnesses believed to be gunshots, along with thirteen other police officers pursued two unarmed Black motorists—Timothy Russell and Malissa Williams—in a high-speed car chase that ended after the officers had discharged 137 bullets into the suspect's vehicle, killing them both. While such tragedies force communities to draw battle lines, as the resident theologian of his predominantly African American congregation, Johnson has boldly insisted that, in God's vision of beloved community, prophetic activism proves of little value for community restoration if priestly concerns get underprivileged or neglected.

In scripture, the biblical prophets spoke oracles as God's mouthpiece. Speaking and petitioning God on the community's behalf, "the priest's message more explicitly carried a stronger interpretative function of God's activity in the world."[5] What distinguishes this preaching voice from its prophetic counterpart is that the principal emphasis of the priestly voice centers on matters of congregational care, specifically in the aftermath of natural disaster, oppressive life situations, and death. Often through African American priestly preaching the preacher functions as intercessor, guiding individuals into a religious encounter or experience with God. Thus, the preacher's active presence and human speech becomes a psychic, physical, and spiritual healing resource.[6]

Also in Cleveland, in the wake of Brelo's acquittal, Jawanza K. Colvin, successor to Otis Moss Jr. at Olivet Baptist Institutional Church, is pictured in a news article walking arm in arm with representative religious leaders in a

---

5.   Kenyatta R. Gilbert, *The Journey and Promise of African American Preaching* (Minneapolis: Fortress, 2011), 13.

6.   Ibid.

protest march, reminiscent of the portrait of Dr. King leading the march from Selma to Montgomery. Colvin's faith-inspiring messages to his more affluent, Black, multigenerational, four-thousand-member congregation, seek to call church leaders, public officials, and community leaders to assume greater obligation to develop a social consciousness around the work of alleviating human suffering. Namely, the work of curbing excessive policing in Cleveland neighborhoods and challenging unjust systems that endorse oppressive acts.

Weekly, Arkansas pastor-revivalist and Howard Divinity alumnus George Lewis Parks Jr. skillfully entwines prophetic proclamation with celebration in the spirit of the folk revival tradition of Black preaching, both within his parish community and "on the road," otherwise known as "the circuit." Birthed in earnest during the First and Second Great Awakenings of the eighteenth century and preserved by celebrated preachers such as C. L. Franklin, Caesar A. W. Clark, and more contemporarily, Ralph Douglas West Sr. and Marcus D. Cosby, the "chanted or musical sermon" or "whooping" (pronounced "hooping") has fallen out of favor in many quarters.[7] But Parks recovers and brings forward the genius of this important legacy of antiphonal exchange that is widely cherished in the American South but is a vanishing art form lost on the ears of a generation of listeners lacking an appreciation for stirring participant-proclamation. Refusing to abscond his homiletical charge of holding together lamentation and celebration, as interpreter of the Word for our time and place, Parks embodies, in the power of the Spirit, spirit-driven messages that are "contextual, Christological, sacramental, ecclesial, and ethical" and point listeners Godward.[8]

Preacher-expositor John Faison Sr. is the social-media-savvy pastor of Watson Grove Missionary Baptist Church located in South Nashville—a livestreaming congregation, where he integrates evangelical fire and social criticism as his church community's priest. Faison, an intergenerational bridger and committed family man and father of three, boasts a congregational membership of thriving Black families who support his local efforts and national initiatives for repairing families and restoring communities of the underprivileged. Obrien Wimbish, the son of a preacher, serves as youth pastor of the

---

7. See chapter 5 in Adam L. Bond's *The Imposing Preacher: Samuel DeWitt Proctor and Black Public Faith* (Minneapolis: Fortress, 2013) for a thoughtful analysis distinguishing the folk/revival tradition of Black preaching from what he terms "college chapel/lecture preaching," 154–61.

8. Sally A. Brown and Luke A. Powery, *Ways of the Word: Learning to Preach for Your Time and Place* (Minneapolis: Fortress, 2016), 47.

People's Community Baptist Church in Silver Spring, Maryland. With Wimbish serving as spiritual advisor to the congregation's college-bound teens, upward of twenty high school graduates received $1,500 scholarships in 2017 to attend colleges and universities across the nation.

Duke Divinity alumnus and African Methodist Episcopal pastor William Lamar IV sounds the clarion call for freedom, justice, and equality from the historic pulpit of the 180-year-old Metropolitan A.M.E church in the heart of our nation's capital. In the spirit of Henry McNeal Turner, Martin L. King Jr., and Gardner C. Taylor, Lamar's thunderous preaching, astute reading of politics, and outspoken criticism of social policies that foster health, educational, and economic inequality for people of color, bespeaks of an unbroken legacy between him and the denomination's founder, Bishop Richard Allen. For Lamar, biblical and theological reflection cannot end in the pulpit. The work of the church must matter on the ground and be intellectually stimulating for his congregation's highly educated laity. James H. Cone's *The Cross and the Lynching Tree*, Howard Thurman's *Jesus and the Disinherited*, Kelly Brown Douglas's *Stand Your Ground*, Obery Hendricks's *The Politics of Jesus*, and Michelle Alexander's *The New Jim Crow* are representative works read by attendees of the transformative Bible study he leads weekly.

Although these emerging clerics may be less known to the general public, they are at the forefront, shaping the discourse for future generations, speaking truth to power to provide new insights about what it means to preach prophetically in postmodern African America and beyond its cultural rim.

A NOTE TO THE READER

Exodus Preaching is intended to be an uncomplicated treatment of its subject matter. As the stress is on the practical, documentation has been kept to a minimum.

The conceptual framework is founded upon *three* biblical touchstones that have defined and refined African American ministers' prophetic voice:

1. The Exodus narrative

2. The prophetic literature

3. The incarnational and messianic witness of Jesus Christ

The book's chapters are organized around four characteristic marks of African American prophetic preaching (*Exodus preaching*) and guided by four reflection questions quietly running in the background.

Four Characteristic Marks

Interpreting the gospel in a present-future sense based on the principles of justice, prophetic preaching:

1. unmasks systemic evil and deceptive human practices by means of moral suasion and subversive rhetoric;

2. remains interminably hopeful when confronted with human tragedy and communal despair;

3. connects the speech act with just actions as concrete praxis to help people freely participate in naming their reality; and

4. carries an impulse for beauty in its use of language and culture.[9]

Four Reflection Questions

1. What is going on in prophetic preaching today?

2. Why is practical guidance on prophetic preaching needed?

3. What ought this guidance resemble in order to be useful for working and aspirant preachers?

4. How might sermon-crafting strategies and the collective voices of emerging African American clerics be an apt resource for those who dare to discover and reclaim their prophetic voice in our times?

Finally, regarding the last question, featured in this work are sermons and sermon excerpts that thematically coincide with a characteristic mark of *Exodus*

---

9. See Gilbert, *A Pursued Justice,* for a more comprehensive treatment of these discourse features.

preaching. However, as a caution, it is important to note that the crafting strategies explored in this book are often but not necessarily tied to a particular biblical touchstone or characteristic mark per se. Thus, some of the crafting strategies may be based solely on the rhetorical dynamics and theological content from the sermon segment being spotlighted. The book is divided into two parts. Featured in this volume are sermon segments and homiletical suggestions of a theoretical sort.

The book's creative hook is its impulse to speak to the fragmentation in curricular resources in the discipline of homiletics, as humanity has entered a new global reality marked by radical pluralism with all of its complexity. The postmodern challenge of Christian theology (preaching in this case) is to achieve the status of "global theology," which is reached through truth-bearing contextual theologies that unify the theological enterprise and allow it to speak from contexts of particularity and to the particularities of diverse contexts and extend to the concerns and contexts of a rapidly changing global environment. For this reason, *Exodus Preaching* seeks to address the singular topic of prophetic preaching multidimensionally, with sensitivity to differences in social location, gender orientation, approaches to scripture, theological viewpoints, ministerial formation, and denominational affiliation among featured clergy, as opposed to exploring the topic on a single axis. Because ministry is often done at the margins, beyond the institutional church proper, *Exodus Preaching* is written not only for highly visible working clergy expected to preach the Word each Sunday but also for ministers serving churches in auxiliary capacities who preach occasionally or do so in non-parish settings. With the evolving ecclesial terrain of our current environment, the title "minister" or "preacher" has shifted to signify more than senior pastor. I am especially sympathetic to the church-groomed itinerants who, like myself, find themselves in familiar and unfamiliar pulpits on any given Sunday. While undoubtedly standards of religious credentialing affirming the community's blessing of the minister's call through licensure or ordination must be upheld, discerning the particulars of one's specific assignment as proclaimer is crucial to having a fruitful preaching life.

My intent is to strike a productive balance between my theorist self and practitioner self. Writing to aid accessibility is important to me but often a tormenting church-versus-academy rivalry happens within. Nevertheless, I take comfort in the fact that my thinking about prophetic preaching has been birthed and nurtured in the cradle of Black Christian practice, shaped by my own theological and confessional commitments, academic exposures, preaching experience(s), and guided by my earnest intent to bolster the health and wellness of African American churches, schools, and communities—identity-shaping contexts from whom I have incurred the greatest personal debt and to whom am I most accountable.

What follows are sermons, crafting strategies gathered from the collective wisdom of some of the most imaginative and creative African American ministers preaching today. I hope you will read through the lens of your own storied reality, which is never absent of contradiction, mercy, and grace. More importantly, I hope you keep an open mind to the end of feeling obligated to raise your prophetic voice in the work of rebuffing systems, practices, and policies that devalue the dignity and worth of all persons.

HOW TO USE THIS BOOK

This book is meant to be a practical resource for ministry leaders (formally and informally trained), seminarians, social justice activists, ministers-in-training groups, musical artists, and general readers interested in the subject matter. The book is comprised of six chapters. Each chapter uses a common template and offers the reader:

- Chapter Introduction

- Crafting Strategies (ways to approach sermon-crafting)

- Crafting Strategy Techniques (CST) (techniques, methods, and tactics for implementing the crafting strategies)

- Thorns and Thistles (warnings and cautions for preaching)

- Sermons associated with Crafting Strategies

- Exercise (to help the reader implement a technique, practice a skill, or explore a crafting strategy further)

The reader should consider keeping a journal or notebook handy to do the exercises at the end of each chapter. Chapters 2–5 are distinct in that each of these chapters is devoted to one of the four characteristic marks of Exodus

Preaching. Finally, in chapter 6, I commend a practical plan with sermon development exercises and then lending my own sermonic voice I analyze a sermon I've preached, using a sermon analysis rubric based on the Four Characteristic Marks of the Exodus Preaching Paradigm. With this in mind, the reader might consider revisiting her or his own previously preached sermons using the rubric as a diagnostic key for their own sermonic analysis.

There is no right or wrong way to approach this book. One might read it from cover to cover and set it aside. Another might simply think about the crafting techniques and reference them again and again as a refresher. Some will sit with the sermons—most of which can be viewed online—examining the way in which the preacher crafts the message and study their techniques. Others will work through the exercises in intergenerational or peer discussion groups. And still others will make use of the Four Tasks sermon plan in chapter 6, in the event he or she is called upon to prepare a sermon.

Chapter One

EXODUS IMAGERY AND SERMONIC PERFORMANCE

In every crisis God raises up a Moses . . . especially where the destiny of [God's] people is concerned.

—C. L. Franklin[1]

Exodus preaching (African American prophetic preaching) is concrete and daring discourse that names God and offers a vision of divine purpose. Preaching of this kind serves an emancipatory agenda. Through criticism and symbols of hope about what God intends and expects of God's human creation, Exodus preaching lands on the ear of the despairing and is dedicated to help them interpret their situation in light of God's justice and the quest for human freedom. As long as people desire to be free, Martin King's insightful query will never ring hollow.

King once asked, "Who is it that is supposed to articulate the longings of people more than the preacher?" Such a question hoists a burden upon every minister who hopes to do something of consequence in partnership with God. To shun the beckoning task of preparing listeners to stand and be counted as co-participants with a promise-bearing God at work in the world is to tighten Egypt's grip and undermine a several-centuries-old quest for freedom. The Exodus saga's correspondence with today's victims of history has added legitimacy to the preacher's speech about God's will toward justice.

---

1. Quotation taken from C. L. Franklin's sermon "Moses at the Red Sea" in *Give Me This Mountain*, ed. Jeff Todd Titon (Urbana: University of Illinois Press, 1989), 107–8.

1

Likewise, the Hebrew prophet's evocative cries for moral accountability to God and community beckons preachers toward high standards of moral and ethical responsibility, just as the salvific agenda and incarnational witness of Jesus remind preachers that the vocation of prophetic truth-telling often co-occurs with personal suffering. Such orienting biblical touchstones invite today's preacher-prophets to stand against the forces of death and evil in both the public square and the church. This is why the enduring pursuit for human dignity and overcoming spiritual and social forces that work against the collective good and welfare of all persons remain so important. In today's culture of trauma and numbness, if the preacher is silent potential pathways to human flourishing will be blocked.

But what might these pathways resemble? I have argued elsewhere that prophetic proclamation is not self-generated discourse but summoned Word taking its beginning and ending in God.[2] Yet because preaching is both a divine and human activity, which calls upon a preacher's gifts and faculties, I believe that strategies to push a preacher to stretch her theological imagination can aid the preacher's growth, especially as it relates to developing a prophetic consciousness, given the current state of the world.

—CRAFTING STRATEGY: PREACHING THE EXODUS NARRATIVE (OR PREACHING FROM THE OLD TESTAMENT)—

Preaching from the Old Testament is just as important as preaching from the New Testament. In fact, if one bypasses or gives surface treatment to the Hebrew scriptures, taken on their own terms, one cannot obtain an appropriate picture of Jesus Christ. That which binds the two testaments together are the promises of God made in the Old Testament (or the Hebrew Bible for the canonically persnickety), which find fulfillment in God's Son in the New Testament witness. Nevertheless, preaching from the Old Testament poses great challenges and openings for the preacher in sermon creation.

Passage selection, understanding of the genre and history of the text, plot sequence and movement, assessment of the rhetorical situation, contemporary relevance, correspondence with the New Testament, pairing exegesis with imagination, and addressing theological problems the selected passage or book present are all of great consequence for sermon creation. Lone-ranger ap-

---

2. Kenyatta R. Gilbert, *A Pursued Justice: Black Preaching from the Great Migration to Civil Rights* (Waco, TX: Baylor University Press, 2016), 6.

proaches to managing these components ensure that the preacher, no matter how earnest, will do violence to the integrity of the chosen passage's claim(s) and discernible intent.

THORNS AND THISTLES: THE CONQUEST NARRATIVES

The conquest narratives that signal the ending of Israel's long march to the promised land can be particularly troublesome for preachers because opposite God's love and mercy toward Israel are God's punitive actions and merciless response toward Israel's foreign foes. To satisfy divine-purpose militarism, genocide, and ethnocentrism, find divine endorsement.

How then might the preacher engage such passages prophetically without suppressing what they clearly state?

The preacher might raise questions and concerns in the sermon itself about inappropriate contemporary appropriations of such texts when made in the name of Jesus Christ. Naming the historical trouble spot and discussing how it contradicts or disregards the core claims of Christian confession in light of Jesus's inaugural vision as recorded in Luke 4:16-21 is a crucial first step.

CST1: ACKNOWLEDGE THE PROBLEM.

Consider this phrasing as a sermon opening:

We often cherry-pick or conveniently jump over biblical passages that rub us the wrong way. To do this is only natural because we need things to line up, don't we? To make rational sense. But what if they don't? What if they offend our Christian sensibilities and refuse to be bullied into what we want them to say? Do we just gather our marbles and run away from them? Do we throw them into our theological waste bins without discussion? I should hope not. I hope we would wrestle a bit with the Whys? and How comes? You do realize that God respects and remains unintimidated by whatever manner of question we can bring to God.

Why would God decree an invasion tactic that endorses the indiscriminate killing of men, women, and children and hold Israel accountable if she does not sign onto the death warrant's dotted line? Perhaps we should chalk this up to the mysterious intentions of God. Or might we make peace with the fact that seeing this as God's act on Israel's behalf and to not see this as Israel's heroism or expression of her military prowess is the way to size up things? What can be said with reasonable certainty is that these weary nomads are extremely vulnerable and sin prone. Ask Moses.

Who's to say they'd not simply enter a new place and fall prey to the temptation to run to the Canaanite gods without a way being made clear? I can think of better ways to do this. I know you could.

But as much as I want to impose my modern diplomacy and peacemaking strategies onto the ancients, I can't. You can't. We must embrace our discomfort. But that isn't all the Christian can do. The Christian can hold this and other troublesome accounts up to the light of the gospel and see if things line up. This gospel bids me to follow after the love of Jesus, and not Joshua's sword.

CST2: FIND THE MAJOR THEMES.

One effective way to enrich sermon preparation is to focus on key doctrinal themes seen in the passage. Ask yourself, "Is this passage about

- covenant and disobedience,
- promise and fulfillment,
- sin and mercy,
- bondage and deliverance,
- patience and faithfulness, or
- divine sovereignty and commitment?"

Coupling and organizing the sermon around these big themes can be an effective strategy for unearthing the intentions of the text.

CST3: PREPARE A REASONED RESPONSE.

After dealing with the text with critical eyes on the merit of what it speaks literally, ascend from history a bit and try interpreting the passage symbolically. Jeffrey Rogers helpfully suggests two possible responses a preacher might use:

- Relate the battle imagery to the struggle and terrors that every person, believers no exception, may face. These battles might entail enduring bouts with mental suffering or resisting addictive and spiritually crippling behaviors. Moses's words to Joshua, "Be strong and courageous . . . for the LORD your God is with you wherever you go" (Josh 1:9) may find resonance in the life of a listener fearing a future that must be faced with steadfast faith.
- Value the fact that "not every citation of scripture was met with Jesus's approval." One might also wager an appeal based

on Matthew 5:21-22, 33-34, accounts that read: "You have heard that it was said to those in ancient times. . . . But I say to you . . ." One should also take note of John 20:30-31, which attests to the fact that Jesus did many things that weren't recorded in the holy scriptures. As the Gospel of John declares "Jesus did many other signs in the presence of his disciples, which are not written in this book. But these are written so that you may come to believe that Jesus is the Messiah, the Son of God, and that through believing you may have life in his name."[3] So ask yourself this question: If the Bible could have more to say to us then why must I insist on shoving the text into my hermeneutical straitjacket?

CST4: TRUST THE POSTMODERN LISTENER.

Contemporary listeners value the preacher's honest wrestling. The preacher gives voice to God's vision and announces what is seen and heard. But the honest preacher will acknowledge interpretive blind spots. The preacher does well to remember that all "see through a mirror dimly" knowing only in part, and this should not diminish hope because believers are assured that because of God's loving concern for us, all things cloudy in the end become clear (1 Cor 13:12).

SERMONIC EXAMPLE ➡

Raquel St. Clair Lettsome
"Hidden Hope"; Exodus 2:10
Samuel DeWitt Proctor Conference
Drake Hotel
Chicago, IL
2012[4]

New Testament scholar Reverend Dr. Raquel Lettsome, the first woman to serve as the executive minister at the historic St. James African Methodist Episcopal Church in Newark, New Jersey, is author of *Call and Consequences:*

---

3. Cf. Jeffrey S. Roger's essay "The Conquest Narratives" in *The New Interpreter's Handbook of Preaching* (Nashville: Abingdon, 2008), 71–72.

4. Typed manuscript. Original version of sermon delivered at the 2012 Samuel DeWitt Proctor Conference at the Drake Hotel in Chicago, Illinois. Audiovisual recording of revised version of sermon delivered on June 12, 2016, at the *Engle Institute of Preaching*, Princeton Theological Seminary: http://av.ptsem.edu/detailedplayer.aspx?PK=a75c9e02-6c32-e611-b265-0050568c0018.

A Womanist Reading of Mark's Gospel. According to Lettsome, "God not only calls preachers to have a prepared Word, God calls for prepared preachers."[5] The best sermons she has preached, says Lettsome, are those conceived and nurtured out of life's "overflow." Namely, she gathers those sermons that emanate from time spent in prayer and regular, consistent, daily Bible reading, time in fellowship with others, and, equally important, time spent when the physical self is rested. This requires an inverted view of preaching and its preparation, says Lettsome. She contends that the preparation of the preacher can be summarized in one word: discipline.[6]

Her sermon "Hidden Hope" launches from Exodus 2:10, tracking the daring women (Hebrew midwives, mother Jochebed, sister Miriam, and Pharaoh's daughter) who rose up at pivotal moments to secure the future of an endangered man-child, the prophet Moses. Lettsome sets the sermonic stage for drama and suspense, asking the question: Can hope be destroyed? *Now a man from the house of Levi went and married a Levite woman. The woman conceived and bore a son; and when she saw that he was a fine baby, she hid him three months* (Exod 2:1-2).

She assumes her listeners are well-acquainted with the storyline and cast of characters. The sermon unfolds with an artfully sophisticated blending of sociolinguistic biblical criticism, theo-symbolic coding, and pastoral care. The sermon's alliterated title and first segment signal to listeners that the preaching moment will be an exercise in aesthetical creativity.

> We are not paranoid. There really is a plot to destroy us, a plot that requires us to reckon with powers and principalities, rulers of darkness and spiritual wickedness in high places (Eph. 6:12) . . . Truth is, just about all of us have already gone through, know about, and/or survived some assassination attempts in which people or circumstances seem to have conspired against us to kill our joy, peace, sanity, self-esteem, educational aspirations . . . character. Because ultimately the thing on the hit list is our hope. Hope . . . the expectation of a favorable future under God's direction;[7] the expectation that God will fulfill God's promises.

---

5. Raquel A. St. Clair (Lettsome), "Preaching from the Overflow," *More Power in the Pulpit: How America's Most Effective Black Preachers Prepare Their Sermons*, ed. Cleophus J. LaRue (Louisville: Westminster John Knox, 2009), 116.

6. Ibid.

7. P. J. Achtemeier, *Harper's Bible Dictionary* (San Francisco: Harper & Row, 1985).

Because of its inductive movement and narrative outline, Lettsome leaves no useful detail unmanaged in order to set the stage. One might see this sermon distilled in three simple propositions: Hope is important. Faith is futile without it. Hope must be protected.

Lettsome calls persons and principalities that plot our demise "hope assassins." They "destroy dreams and vanquish hopes . . . [and] can fire at point blank range—a word of doubt here, some discouragement there, a roll of the eyes, a carefully placed sigh, or just be close enough to stab us in the back. . . . They fear us even though we have done nothing to them." She continues, "The way we make it through these plots is God hides us. This was the case of Moses."

From this opening hook, Lettsome eases into the text and tells us that Moses was born in the middle of an assassination attempt. She says, "Pharaoh was trying to annihilate all the Hebrew boys so the assassination attempt was not directed against him specifically. It was directed against what he and the other baby boys represented." She shifts into didactic mode, playing up the significance of a "man-child." The man-child, she says, is a generation's hope, the continuation of a people . . . in them, "was housed every unfulfilled dream, every unmet desire."

Pharaoh's strategic plan to annihilate the oppressed Hebrews' hope, she outlines, was to box them, limit their employment prospects, and conscript them into forced labor; confine them to slave status with no rank or respect; and if plan one and two failed, then assassinate them. The sermon's message is unmistakably working on multiple levels, biblically and contextually. Lettsome follows the biblical narrative, but the beauty of her composition is in the sermon's relation to the occasioned event. The theme of the 2012 Proctor Conference was The New Jim Crow Summit, after the release of civil rights attorney Michelle Alexander's *New York Times* bestseller[8] on the subject. Alexander highlights the plight of African American men, arguing that America's political and criminal justice system functions as a redesign of the "Jim Crow" system. Black mass incarceration, she maintains, has forged a racial caste system that permanently bars Black males from any political participation in society upon re-entry. This crisis is problematic because it ensures the

---

8.   Alexander notes that most incarceration arrests are for misdemeanor offenses and further contends that the nation's criminal justice system has never intended to reform the incarcerated; rather, the fundamental goal is capitalistic expansion of industry using tax dollars to obtain cheap labor. Cf. *The New Jim Crow: Mass Incarceration in the Age of Colorblindness* (New York: The New Press, 2012).

further splintering of Black families, as Black ex-convicts re-enter society with few prospects for improving their economic or social station.

But the sermon's thrust does not settle with subversive critique alone. Lettsome pairs criticism with hope. And this hope comes in the form of God typified as mother.

> Jochebed, Moses's mother, gives birth to hope in the midst of the dreadful, hopeless situation. . . . Jochebed gives birth to hope and the midwives let hope live. . . . So Jochebed hides her hope in a basket. In Hebrew, the word for "basket" is literally an "ark." She dares to protect her hope until this flood of trouble is abated. And then Pharaoh's daughter sees her hope, takes pity on her hope, and protects her hope in the palace. . . . And I know we often call God "Father," but sometimes, God is a mother to us like Jochebed. God looks at us and sees brand-new creations, born again by blood and the Holy Spirit but we are still babies in so many ways.

Having named the tragic reality of communal despair and a pathway toward hopeful resolution, she negotiates a christocentric correspondence in sermonic summary—the celebration of the good news that hope can be built on nothing less than Jesus's blood and righteousness. Ending in celebratory fashion, she proclaims:

> In a court of law, prosecution and defense can call witnesses and submit evidence to support their respective cases. While you were hidden, God used you as a witness. God let people watch you to see how God kept you, never left you, no matter what Pharaoh did.

> But one day, God is going to call you out of hiding and present you as evidence. God will use you as Exhibit A to showcase God's anointing. You will be Exhibit B to demonstrate what a breakthrough looks like . . . Exhibit C . . . Exhibit D to show how you enter a new season . . . Ultimately, you will be Exhibit H, a Hidden Hope! And if your hope is in God, you will never be alone. For you have a hidden Savior for every hidden situation. He was hidden:

> In four hundred years of silence when there was no canonical word from the Lord

> In forty-two generations until he was born a babe in Bethlehem

> In Egypt until Herod died

In a borrowed tomb for three days until he rose to stoop no more

In the heavens until he shall reveal himself in all glory, majesty, beauty, and power and we shall behold him for we shall see him as he is. . . . That's why, "our hope is built on nothing less than Jesus's blood and righteousness."

"Hidden Hope" plays well in liturgical settings both congregational and conference-formatted, but religio-cultural sermonic lyricism is restricted neither to traditional modes of homiletic proclamation nor to ecclesial settings where religious speech-acts are typically performed. Creative sermonic discourse arises in response to rhetorical situations that need and invite it, and often amphitheaters, concert halls, and café lounges become the sacred space for the spoken and embodied Word.

—CRAFTING STRATEGY: SETTING UP THE DELAYED HOOK—

This rhetorical strategy cautions the preacher not to say too much too soon. Listeners can read the text for themselves. But it is the preacher's task to speak to shape consciousness and bring the gospel forward as gift and challenge. In fact, from prologue to epilogue, the Exodus story itself unfolds sequentially.

Picking up where the book of Genesis ends, Joseph dies in Egypt along with his generation, the Israelites multiply and grow strong as a people, a new king ascends to the throne but knows not Joseph's legend, and finally, in fear and intimidation the new king sets out to oppress the Israelites and diminish their population. To follow the mind of the narrative is to see that it virtually preaches itself.

As with many good movies, the plot unfolds inductively, hinting all along the way why each character is important to the storyline, noting the obstacles to be overcome, and revealing why God's involvement is necessary. Biblical narratives have plots, twists, and turns, moving from problem to resolution, that make for the stuff of drama. To shape messages that capture today's listener, sermon setup is critical.

A GOOD DELAYED SETUP SHOULD:

1. Capture textual and/or situational intensity and gravity early on to bring text and situation into sharp focus.

9

2. Set up suspense that creates a bind and establishes a burden that listeners hope and expect the gospel to address meaningfully or resolve.

3. Begin with or set up anticipation for a searching or striking question. When logically arranged, the same question used repeatedly throughout the sermon can be used to great effect in engaging the hearer meaningfully. Caution: A preacher should only raise questions if the preacher has planned a well timed, fitting response to follow. Nothing robs the listener of story or sabotages the sermon more than a stream of rhetorical questions only raised for effect.

4. Share a meaning-making scene (s) using vivid language, directional cues, and carefully crafted words.

5. Be rehearsed. The preacher should strive to commit the first and last minute of the sermon to memory. Both should be memorable.

6. Postpone propositions. Propositions that are made too early are killjoys to sermon setup. Often introductory remarks or spending too much time explaining the historical context of the passage robs the preacher of an opportunity to connect with the listener. Nothing slows sermon momentum and attentiveness as tell-all titles and sermon openers like, "The title of my sermon is . . . Or, turn with me to the book of Exodus where it talks about the birth of Moses." Or, fashioned of late and quickly becoming cliché, the preacher says to the congregation after reading the scripture, "touch and tell your neighbor [God is bringing you out of Egypt] and now turn to your other neighbor and say [God is bringing me out of Egypt] . . ." to which the expectation held by the preacher is that this method will somehow make the sermon more memorable when in fact it does four things to the contrary:

   - It forces listeners into another's personal space.
   - It will likely foster inauthentic social interaction between preacher and pew.
   - It unwittingly communicates that the preacher needs the congregation to be won over before some serious wrestling with the scriptures has taken place.
   - It tells listeners at the outset that you don't trust them to get what you are about to talk about.

10

If this is your custom, you may want to think about using this formula sparingly if at all. Some people deeply value opening their own homiletical birthday gift without the preacher or their neighbor telling them what's inside.

Also, postponement tends to be very effective when attempting to address controversial or sensitive topics (e.g., human sexuality, war and patriotism, homosexuality, abortion, women's ordination, euthanasia, mental disorders, over-policing and gun violence, intimate partner violence) that may be hard for listeners to hear but the congregation should address or care about.

7. Have a purposeful function. A sermon can function a number of ways based on sermonic purpose and the sacred text it considers and interprets. The sermon may work by privileging a singular function or combination of them in establishing the sermon's agenda. Will it be best characterized as a teaching (*didache*), exhortative (*paraklesis*), or a parabolic (*parabole*) sermon? Regardless of principal function, ideally the message will shift to a proclamatory (kerygmatic) address.[9]

HIP-HOP LYRICISM AND SERMONIC PERFORMANCE

The cultural production of gospel-infused rap music has made its presence felt in virtually every act of the worship service, from liturgical dance to choral singing to the preached Word, though not without a fair share of theological clumsiness. For an increasing number who fall under the Black Christian canopy, all things liturgical move to the syncopated rhythms of hip-hop and go-go music. Hip-hop music is unique in this way. While theological grammar, religious ideas, and biblical concepts pervade the lyrics of hip-hop social poets, expressly Christian or not, under careful scrutiny, songs performed by so-called secular rappers such as Talib Kweli, Missy Elliot, Kanye West, Remy Ma, Nas, Jay-Z, Mos Def, Kendrick Lamar, and Common reveal that they rarely follow linear logic, and in many instances the religious or theo-symbolic ideas expressed appear disjointed and even contradictory.[10]

---

9. David Bartlett, "Sermon," *Concise Encyclopedia of Preaching*, ed. William Willimon and Richard Lischer (Louisville: Westminster John Knox, 1995), 433–35.

10. Monica R. Miller, "The Promiscuous Gospel: The Religious Complexity and Theological Multiplicity of Rap Music," *Readings in African American Church Music and Worship, Volume 2*, ed. James Abbington (Chicago: GIA Publications, Inc., 2014), 614–15.

Although many of the celebrated hip-hop artists today deploy graphic and morally reprehensible language, there's much to be gained when preachers listen critically to how hip-hop lyricists capture in melodic verse the *ironic* to wage war against the status quo. Urban poets earn a hearing making audacious declarations to lift meaning from the beautiful and tragically ugly underside of life. Using provocative speech and lyrical subversion, many socially conscious artists confound and challenge keepers of the status quo.

SERMONIC EXAMPLE ➡️

Common and John Legend
"Glory," 2014[11]
Dolby Theater
Drake Hotel
Hollywood, CA
2015 Oscars

Common's stunning tribute to the freedom fighters who marched from Selma to Montgomery in 1965 for voting rights protection reveals his fidelity to a socially conscious, justice-oriented strain of rap music. His lyrics disclose the essence of his own spiritual odyssey, theological evolution, and belief that traces of the Spirit reside in all people.[12] Joined by neo-soul balladeer John Legend at the 87th Academy Awards ceremony, Common performed the Oscar-winning musical sermon "Glory." The duo mesmerized the audience with their antiphonal chorus-and-verse exchange. In message and intent, the song marries prophetic criticism with sermonic phrasing. Like the African American spirituals, as sung proclamation, "Glory" voices hope in the face of human tragedy. Following Legend's opening chorus, in rapid and rhythmic pace, Common paints a portrait of lament and celebration—features similar

---

11. "Glory," the theme song for 2014 film *Selma*, earned songwriters Common (Lonnie Lynn), John Legend (John Stephens), and Che Smith Best Original Song at the 2015 Oscars and Golden Globe Awards. Hip-hop artist Common is a south side Chicago native who names Trinity United Church of Christ as his home congregation and Rev. Dr. Jeremiah Wright Jr. his pastor. See "Glory (from the Motion Picture Selma) Oscar Performance," February 23, 2015, YouTube video, 5:20, posted by blacktreetv, https://youtu.be/H9MKXR4gLjQ.

12. Luke A. Powery, *Spirit Speech: Lament and Celebration in Preaching* (Nashville: Abingdon, 2009), 91.

in style to what is known as the chanted folk sermon, first popularized in the slave quarters by "spiritual preachers."[13]

In this first verse, Common hoists graphic imagery of a downcast people with hands raised in humble surrender to God as he states, "Hands to the heaven, no man, no weapon." With this verse, he articulates the often over-spiritualized, frequently voiced line of scripture, "no weapon formed against me shall prosper" (see Isa 54:17), as his text.

Contemporary Black gospel artist Fred Hammond's "No Weapon" further etched this phrase in the musical consciousness of many Black Christians. This textual reference provides the biblical-theological-hermeneutical key to the sermon's logic, whose running thread depicts the indomitability of the human spirit in search of what Luke Powery calls the "divine wind."[14] Despite spiritual warfare and the sins of racial hatred perpetrated against everyday people, Common maintains that God honors human suffering and ultimately redeems it, so even in the worst of situations, God can turn those situations into blessings. With impeccable timing and lyrical precision, Common describes a kind of justice he wants to see in the world—justice that honors cultural particularity.

One can hear this impulse in Common's trouble-making wordplay, "Justice for all just ain't specific enough," recalling verses of the Pledge of Allegiance, as he speaks to the unfulfilled promise of true democracy for Blacks. In the verses following, he assails the nation's self-deceit and decries its unjust practices. He infers that to cling to the garbs of religious piety without concrete, just actions to follow, is to nurture a false testimony that mocks the meaning of Christ's public crucifixion, the importance of Rosa Parks's courage to sit down in a seat forbade her, and that trivializes the death of the unarmed teen Michael Brown, who was fatally shot in Ferguson, Missouri, by Darren Wilson, the legally exonerated White police officer who escaped indictment.

In verse 2, Selma becomes a metaphor for freedom fighting past and present. Here Common unmasks the horrors of systemic evils visited upon

---

13. Luke A. Powery, *Dem Dry Bones: Preaching, Death, and Hope* (Minneapolis: Fortress, 2012), 23–24. In concert with rhetorician Bruce Rosenberg's study of African American folk preaching, Powery makes a distinction between "spiritual preaching" and "manuscript preaching." Cf. Bruce Rosenberg, *Can These Bones Live? The Art of the American Folk Preacher* (Urbana: University of Illinois Press, 1988).

14. Luke A. Powery, *Spirit Speech: Lament and Celebration in Preaching* (Nashville: Abingdon, 2009), 91.

Black life through Jim Crow's deceptive "separate but equal" doctrine. For poetic effect, Common conflates past and present events into a synthesized whole. The song affirms the fact that racial progress has occurred, but given recent events that have played out in places like Ferguson, New York, and Baltimore, the freedom, justice, and equality for which King lived and died still eludes society's most vulnerable citizens. Common's spoken truths about human suffering—that which remains unfinished in America's land of promise—reaches perfect crescendo in John Legend's hope-filled outro, "When the glory comes," that is, God's glorious in-breaking, "When the war is won, when it's all said and done . . . We'll cry glory, oh glory." Through the balladeer's glory cry resounds the call for a form of justice that gives birth to hope. In the end, taking the form of melodic hip-hop artistry, Legend's vocals and Common's Kingian lyricism link song to circumstance to render a transformative vision of hope in the face of collective misery and human suffering.

—CRAFTING STRATEGY: USING METAPHORS (THINK POETRY, NOT PROSE)—

To do so is to honor a world-yet-to-be. No figurative device is quite as powerful for stimulating thought as the metaphor. Metaphors are generative because they associate two distinct things; that is, one thing is the representation of another, and helps people to see things in a new light. As with most any literary device involving the use of language, metaphors depart from their literal meaning to create an image or picture in the mind of the listener. What this advice suggests is that the use of metaphor accomplishes complex rhetorical tasks that literal language cannot.

How can we incorporate, organize, and assess the strength and character of our metaphoric constructions?

M. Osborn groups metaphors into *eleven* metaphorical families:

- Water and Sea
- Light and Dark
- The Human Body
- War
- Structures

- Animals

- The Family

- Above and Below

- Forward and Backward

- Natural Phenomena

- Sexuality[15]

Consider the following examples of rhetorical construction from the illustrated sermons above in relation to their metaphorical family based on the illustrated sermons above:

- *The Human Body:* Common—saw the face of Jim Crow under a bald eagle

- *War:* Lettsome—". . .just about all of us have already gone through, know about, and/or survived some assassination attempts in which people or circumstances seem to have conspired against us to kill our joy, peace, sanity, self-esteem, educational aspirations . . . character. Because ultimately the thing on the hit list is our hope . . ."

- *The Family:* Common—born again by blood

- *Sexuality:* Lettsome—"Jochebed, Moses's mother, gives birth to hope."

15. M. Osborn, *Orientations to Rhetorical Style* (Chicago: Science Research Associates, 1976). Cited in Roderick P. Hart, *Modern Rhetorical Criticism*, 2nd ed. (Boston: Allyn & Bacon, 1996), 147–48. Also see George Lakoff and Mark Johnson, *Metaphors We Live By* (Chicago: University of Chicago Press, 2003).

➡ **EXERCISE** ⬅

Look at a sermon you have preached and underline each metaphor or simile you see. If there are not any present, you need to use more imagination as you craft.

Start with similes and then metaphor (e.g., the love of God is like finding a new door after an open door is shut; sinners live like tomorrow is in the bank; peace is a river stilled by a sovereign wind tamer; Judah is a roaring lion).

Exodus preaching expands the sacred imagination of the listener. Martin L. King Jr. used mental pictures to help downtrodden listeners to see what he saw on his metaphoric Mt. Nebo at Canaan's edge. Instead of a singular reliance on patterns in ordinary prose, preacher-poets communicate in signs and symbols that explode the dimensions through which a listener may encounter God in the preached Word. Though divergent in sermonic presentation, what the arresting performances of King, Lettsome, and Common hold in common is an agenda that seeks to address the social dislocation of a journeying Afro-Atlantic people forever negotiating the uneven terrain of their Egypto-American experience. For them, petitionary truth-telling remains the vehicle but hope remains the nomadic telos.

UNMASKING EVIL AND DETHRONING IDOLS

If you are neutral in situations of injustice, you have chosen the side of the oppressor.

—Desmond Tutu

Moses is the archetypal prophet of the Jewish faith tradition. A pre-exilic prophet, "slow of tongue," Moses had inherited a very different religious landscape than his sixth-, seventh-, and eighth-century successors—Amos, Habakkuk, and Jeremiah. Knowing this is compass setting for any Christian preacher who would preach prophetically. Having a working knowledge of the social world and the ways in which the Hebrew prophets' words of judgment and hope addressed nation, monarchs, and foreign foes is essential.

The prophets' task was to communicate God's instruction, and theirs was the audacious task of unmasking systemic evil and deceptive, self-serving human practices in a dangerous social world. For this work, Moses used the gift of moral suasion to persuade the Israelites that he was God's representative, and as God's mouthpiece, he spoke subversively to dismantle Pharaoh's empire. Put succinctly, Moses, the servant of Yahweh, was peerless in the task of speaking truth to power.

Exodus preaching unmasks systemic evil and deceptive human practices by means of moral suasion and subversive rhetoric.

Duke University dean of chapel and homiletics scholar Luke Powery rightly asserts: "What is inside preachers is just as important as what comes outside of preachers through words and actions."[1] If Jesus took moments to retreat and pray, he argues, why haven't homiletics classrooms and texts accented prayer's vital role for preaching? Prophetic preaching is God-summoned discourse, and to hear God insist on preachers nurturing and nourishing their devotional life. When preaching is not guided by prayer, preachers and, by implication, those who listen on, seldom hear a voice outside of their own.

An effectual preaching life is the fruit of a prayerful daily life.

—CRAFTING STRATEGY: CONSIDERING THE LECTIONARY—

CST 1: USE THE LECTIONARY FOR HOMILETICAL FOCUS.

Too often preachers rush to preach from their favorite texts while disregarding others just as important—this is the predominant strategy of African American preachers who did not grow up in what is commonly referred to as "high church" liturgical traditions. But there's great value to be discovered using the Revised Common Lectionary (RCL) as a preaching resource. Using the lectionary urges preachers toward more thoughtful biblical and theological reflection. Through it one has an inbuilt homiletical roadmap from week to week, which aids in pre-planning. The RCL coincides with the Christian year. Thus, using it provides preachers at least two helpful safeguards. It ensures that preachers are not preaching a Christmas message on Easter or Pentecost Sundays, but will be seasonally in sync with preachers in faith communities beyond one's own listening to the same listing of biblical texts. Moreover, it encourages the preacher to preach the whole counsel of scripture, even texts that disturb the preacher's psyche or afflict comfortable hearers.

---

1. Sally A. Brown and Luke A. Powery, *Ways of the Word* (Minneapolis: Fortress, 2016), 51.

THORNS AND THISTLES: HELPS NOT HANDCUFFS (PART 1)

Obviously, as with any planning method, a preacher can become handcuffed, and may, if slavishly relied on, stifle the move of the Spirit and scapegoat issues that need to readily be addressed.

Comparable to the "preacher's choice" method, even with the lectionary, preachers might unduly privilege a certain genre of texts for preaching. For example, some denominational traditions expect the preacher to preach exclusively from the Gospel lesson. A few will run to the prophetic literature if they have a particular axe to grind; some will run to the epistles if they want their congregants to behave in a certain way; others wade through the Psalms if attempting to help people process pain or celebrate God's blessings; others will run to the Old Testament narratives for their colorful stories, and daring others will set their interpretive focus on the apocalyptic texts to catch a glimpse of the future.

In his sermon "The Other Jesus," Powery declares that a domesticated Jesus under human control is a savior of our making who bears no resemblance to the Jesus attested to in scripture. Paradox is the disruptively powerful subversive rhetorical device Powery deploys to prick the conscience and stir the imagination of the university congregation where he ministers. On the liturgical calendar, the message was thematically based on Jesus's transfiguration and delivered on Transfiguration Sunday.

CST2: PAY ATTENTION TO THE PARADOXICAL.

Paradoxical preaching unearths the incongruities of human experience and compels listeners to reorient and reset their thinking about a mysterious God in a taken-for-granted world. This is what Luke Powery accomplishes in his sermon "The Other Jesus."

SERMONIC EXAMPLE →

Luke A. Powery
"The Other Jesus"; Matthew 17:1-9
Transfiguration Sunday
Duke University Chapel
Durham, North Carolina
2014[2]

---

2. Used by permission of Dr. Luke A. Powery. "Sunday Service – 3/2/14 – Luke Powery," March 4, 2014, YouTube video, 1:17:53, posted by DukeChapel, https://youtu.be/FYstEbK0xWs?list=PL-FG5VqyzZtXbQYNJDGcYZRdVxoOY_XWI.

SERMON: "THE OTHER JESUS"; MATTHEW 17:1-9

Jesus is other. He is not one of us. He is not our best friend, our BFF, our bosom buddy, plopped down in our living room on a sofa, drinking a cold one or two with us, while we watch Duke defeat Syracuse and see their coach lose his mind on the basketball court (though that was pretty sweet). This may surprise you but Jesus was not praying for Duke or Syracuse to win. He didn't go to a cross for NCAA basketball championships. He had other things on his mind and on his face.

On a mountain, he's transfigured before the inner circle of disciples (Peter, James, and John) "and his face shone like the sun, and his clothes became dazzling white." If they didn't realize then that Jesus was other, Moses and Elijah show up and talk with him through a Holy Spirit Skype. You would think the disciples would understand what was happening because it's not every day the representatives of the Law and the Prophets show up with Jesus to form a holy triumvirate. But Peter doesn't really seem to get it.

Though he has this vision, he has limited vision. He volunteers to make three dwellings—one for Jesus, Moses, and Elijah. One could read this as a sign of hospitality but one may also read it as signifying a form of hostility. Peter not only wants to be in the presence of Jesus and the others, but he wants to control what they live in as if they can be enclosed. I'll make you a dwelling. I'll domesticate Jesus as if Jesus is one of us, like us, desiring a fine home, a companion, and at least one dog, hopefully like my buddy, Randolph. Peter, like us, becomes so used to a domesticated Jesus that we think we can make the parameters of his dwelling when in fact he's really our spiritual home. Jesus will not be confined by our human limitations and constructs.

He is not one of us. He is other. He's not made in our image or denominational heritage, race, gender, or class. We may want Jesus to be a Blue Devil but Jesus is not a shadow of ourselves in the reflection of our light. We are called to reflect his transfiguration glory and light.

And just when we thought we understood Jesus because we saw him as one of us, just when we think we have him under control, just when he's become so cool and safe that we can wear him on a bracelet or necklace, just when we've made him into our image, he changes his appearance and is transfigured to make us know that he is God and not our traditions or theologies or even chapel buildings. Jesus will not be idolized or made into an idol because he is a living, holy, and wholly other God. Just when we think we know what he looks like and how he always acts, his appearance changes and he becomes other because he wants us to change our way of thinking about him and that which is other.

During the much-heated era of what was called "the worship wars" within the church, people argued about what type of music should be used in worship—traditional or contemporary; pipe organ or a band with guitars; hymns or praise songs. Some of you may have scars from that battle! I believe we've moved beyond this battleground into a more mature time but as it relates to worship, writer Annie Dillard reminds us that we are like "children playing on the floor with their chemistry sets, mixing up a batch of TNT to kill a Sunday morning." Not the most generous perspective on humans at worship and the truth is that we haven't always been generous toward each other, especially during these past worship wars. I had a former seminary professor, who shall go unnamed; he called praise songs "7/11 songs"—they had seven words that were repeated eleven times. He claimed they were so simple that his dog could sing them. One may agree with his liturgical taste but at the same time just because he didn't like it didn't mean Jesus wasn't pleased with it or glorified by it.

That musical genre was other thus he felt that he could denigrate it and by doing so, implicitly dismiss the worship life of thousands of Christians in this country and the world. Christian worship was in his cultural and theological image and anything outside of his intellectual dwelling was not deemed worthy. Underneath this liturgical elitism was either an arrogance or fear that God may move and act in ways we would never approve. God is not made in our image.

Jesus is transfigured before the disciples to show that otherness and change and difference are really okay. It is a reminder that no one tradition, culture, or community has a monopoly on Christ, Christian identity, and practice. Usually, we hear about things or places or people being *othered* but here Jesus others himself to demonstrate that he will not be entombed and trapped in our myopic thinking. He is not chiseled into theological limestone or dogma because he is free and on the loose in the world and in our lives, saying and doing things we may consider to be unsophisticated and inappropriate for a God. And look at what Jesus does that is considered the folly of the gospel—he dies on a cross; this is unacceptable for a Messiah. Jesus is not one of us. He is other. He is not attached to our umbilical cord. We did not give birth to him; he wants to be born in us. And like any birth, it involves pain.

Because he is other, the inevitable happens and is what happens to the other many times. His transfiguration occurs in the context of the prediction of his suffering and death. His gaze is turned toward Jerusalem, the place of his death, reminding us that he didn't come to make us successful. He came to save us by a cross and to encourage us to join him in suffering and death. As I've seen on Twitter and heard this week in a post-lecture Q&A, "the only place success comes before work is in the dictionary." Jesus redefines success through his cruciform work of redemption. This is not the Jesus the disciples bargained for; he is an-other Jesus whose trajectory of success is to die, not to live in a confining dwelling we make. Jesus faces his other, Death itself, head on.

His end shouldn't surprise us because when someone is other, all kinds of horrific things can happen. The other can easily be written out of the pages of humanity because they play loud music in their SUV or wear a hoodie. Their hair, their clothes, their religion, their race, their gender, their sexual orientation is different, therefore we may demonize them because we deem them other than ourselves and count them as subhuman, even bully them into suicide, an unnecessary crucifixion just because they are not made in our selfsame image or cannot be housed in our dwelling. "Violence stems from the denial of Otherness" (Gideon Ofrat). French philosopher Jacques Derrida teaches that any tradition, system, person, or concept that closes off the possibility of the other is poison and may lead to the death of the other. They will know we are Christians by our love, not by how much others believe what we do or act like we do.

Yet we can't help but worship a Jesus that we think looks like us. We have a White Jesus and a Black Jesus, a Mexican immigrant Jesus, a Chinese Jesus, a muscular Jesus with a six-pack, a laughing Jesus, a Rasta Jesus, a mini-me Jesus. We make him into our image but the transfiguration reveals that Jesus is not only other but he refuses to be made into an idol that can be controlled and easily disregarded and discarded. You can't ignore his sunshiny face and dazzling clothes. But just in case, there's no way to miss the voice that speaks out of the bright cloud and sets the record straight about who Jesus is. There's still something within us that wants to claim full knowledge of Jesus but we can't fully know.

We only see through a glass dimly because he is other, not the blond-haired blue-eyed Jesus on the church fan or the one depicted in our Sunday school material or even the middle-eastern Jewish man with a beard from the BBC special about Jesus. We must admit that as other, Jesus may not be what we think and perhaps not what we want many times because what we really want is a Jesus who fits into our dwelling and our plans.

But his otherness calls us to spiritual openness in seeing difference dazzle on the face of God. Difference as the light of God. Not self-sameness but otherness as the glory of God on the earth when it has been touched by transfiguration. But this transfiguration strikes terror in the hearts of the disciples. They are overcome by fear once they hear "this is my Son, the Beloved; with him I am well pleased; listen to him!" It's as if they can't believe this transfigured person is really Jesus, the Messiah, because this was not the Jesus they signed up to follow. If they couldn't believe with their own eyes, now they couldn't believe with their own ears.

Fear brings them to their knees because often we fear what we don't understand or what we've never experienced because it was not our tradition or custom or *our* Jesus. Maybe we're so used to a fossilized and impotent Jesus that is on display in a medieval museum only to be viewed and not obeyed, and definitely not to be followed to a cross. This other Jesus scares us because he's not the one we grew up with or heard about. This other Jesus causes our "citadels of certainties" to become "sand castles" (James Olthius). Thus, anything different, anything other, makes us afraid.

I'm currently teaching a class on Howard Thurman, former dean of the chapels at Howard and Boston Universities. *Life* magazine rated him as one of the most important religious leaders in the United States in 1953. In his 1949 classic book *Jesus and the Disinherited*, he says that people are "hounded by day and harrowed by night because of some fear." Fear, he writes, is a "persistent hound of hell." Let's be real. Happiness was not listed as an essential trademark of any disciple. Ironically, fear should be noted as a trait on a disciple's résumé.

The disciples don't teem with confidence in Matthew. When a windstorm arose on the sea and the boat was being swamped by waves, Jesus asks them, "Why are you afraid?" (Matt 8:26). When Jesus walks on water, the disciples are terrified and think he's a ghost and cry out in fear (Matt 14:26). Peter starts walking on the water too, but when he became frightened he begins to sink (Matt 14:30). Fear can drown you if all you have known is a Jesus who is made in your image. The other Jesus, the transfigured one, can be spooky because we always thought he was one of us, just a long-time member in our neighborhood church.

But this mountaintop experience reveals that Jesus is other and may do some things that we would never approve and be someone we never really knew because we only knew the one in our dwelling. This Jesus may be alien to us because he's not even an orthodox God. So we fear the other, the unknown, that which is not us, on the other side of the border, the other side of a political issue. The other is viewed as a potential danger.

We fear because we don't trust God enough that even when Jesus changes before our eyes and becomes other, we are afraid. We're afraid that Jesus's metamorphism may actually tell us how uncomfortable we are with the other, ourselves, and with change. So uncomfortable that even when God acts in ways we've never experienced we believe it can't possibly be God because it hasn't happened in our existential universe. We construct a wall of fear and call names like "illegal," "unorthodox," or "heretic." Other.

Despite the name-calling and fear, the transfigured Jesus reveals that the other does not have to be scary but should be engaged and desires to be known. The other can bring comfort and calm if you get close enough. Here, it is Jesus, who is other, who actually reaches out to the disciples and touches them and tells them not to be afraid. The transfiguration rejects a religion of fear and the touch of transfiguration may actually change us as well by recognizing that the other does not need to be feared but represents unforeseeable possibilities and unexpected gifts. The other is not always a foe but can be a friend and what the transfiguration reveals is that it may even be the Christ.

"Let the other come!" (Derrida) Embrace difference. Embrace the other, whatever or whomever it may be because it is in the "drama of embrace" (Miroslav Volf) that you will experience the luminous presence of God.

CST3: EXPOSE THE IRONIC.

As a rhetorical device, the ancient Greeks used feigned ignorance or "irony" as a disruptive force to expose a contradiction between circumstance and expectation. The prophets of scripture waged linguistic assault on the keepers of status quo with stinging confrontation, but Walter Brueggemann rightly suggests that in our current social reality, the replication of the old confrontational model of prophet versus king "is increasingly difficult to bring off . . .

because it assumes that the 'prophetic voice' has enough clout, either social or moral, to gain a hearing."[3] Brueggemann adds, "Given [our] social reality . . . I suspect whatever is 'prophetic' must be more cunning and more nuanced and perhaps ironic."

CST4: TRY STORIED APPROACHES.

Point structure still has a place in preaching, but wooden point structure should be banished to the homiletical carpenter's woodshed. After revealing the sermon's theme on the nature of idolatry in his message, inductively, Jonathan L. Walton moves his listeners from one illustrative vignette to the next pairing biblical commentary, historical research, biography, reflective social criticism, and song lyrics as a way to reinforce his sermon's prophetic agenda and create organic flow. Ostensibly, the listener will not remember every illustration cited in the sermon, but what will stick are the shared scenes, anecdotes, illustrative slice of life, and theme under consideration, which appears to be the goal.

SERMONIC EXAMPLE ⏩

Jonathan L. Walton
"The Idolatry of Injustice"; John 2:14-16
The Memorial Church of Harvard University
Cambridge, MA
2015[4]

SERMON: "THE IDOLATRY OF INJUSTICE," JOHN 2:14-16

On the night of March 7, 1965, people up and down the East Coast sat captivated in front of their black and white television sets. Bostonians, New Yorkers, and Atlantans watched actor Spencer Tracy play Judge Haywood in the network premier of *Judgment of Nuremberg*. In this 1961 Academy Award–winning motion picture, Tracy's character is trying to figure out something. Judge Haywood is trying to figure out how so many Germans could either ignore or remain silent concerning the crimes of the Nazi regime. Tracy's character is trying

---

3.   Walter Brueggemann, *The Prophetic Imagination*, 2nd ed. (Minneapolis: Fortress, 2001), xii.

4.   Original manuscript used by permission. Sermon was delivered in Cambridge, Massachusetts, on March 3, 2015.

to figure out how everyday German people—folks who were neither fanatics nor sociopaths—could follow Hitler down such a despicable drain of death and human destruction. And Tracy's character, Judge Haywood, was trying to wrap his mind around what Hannah Arendt would ultimately refer to as the "banality of evil"—injustice fueled not by a particular ideology as much as by an uncritical acceptance and indifference to human suffering.

This is why Tracy asked probing questions to a married German couple who were serving him an evening meal. "You're good people," Tracy declared, "but you must have been aware of what was going on."

To this the wife replied, "We are little people . . . we don't get into politics . . . Hitler did some good things. He built the Autobahn. He gave more people work. But the other things . . . the things he did to the Jews and the rest . . . we knew nothing about it." Then the husband adds, "And if we did know, what could we do?"

And right when Tracy took a deep breath to ponder the sincerity yet naivety of the couple's statement, ABC News interrupted the movie. It was an interruption that could have been orchestrated by the archangels due to its topic and timing. Grainy camera footage captured horrific images in Selma, Alabama. Sheriff Jim Clark and his deputized Ku Klux Klansmen had savagely attacked an assembly of peaceful protesters on the Edmund Pettus Bridge.

This protest was organized by young activists James Bevel, John Lewis, and Diane Nash. And this protest was populated by courageous Selma citizens like Amelia Boynton—people who decided that they would no longer remain silent in the face of evil and injustice; people who decided that they would no longer resign to second-class citizenship as a result of being denied the right to vote; people who through the storm of segregation and the dark night of political disenfranchisement declared, "We are sick and tired of being sick and tired."

This is why they sought to march from Selma to Montgomery. They wanted to let the nation and world know that the status quo was no longer sufficient. Unfortunately, their collective courage and justifiable claims of democracy were met with tear gas, billy clubs, and Jim Clark's own cattle prod. So on this day—a day that would go down in history as "Bloody Sunday"—the world was forced to witness how far a southern state government would go to preserve and protect its exclusive claims to power.

And I believe it to be a divinely inspired coincidence that on this third Sunday of Lent, the Gospel lesson of John speaks to this very issue—challenging structural systems of power. We read the lesson for your hearing. Jesus, in preparation for the feast of the Passover, headed to the temple in Jerusalem. He is angered by what he finds outside the gates. People were selling cattle, sheep, and doves on the temple grounds. There were also moneychangers—men who had booths open to exchange currency from faraway lands.

It is important to understand the context here. Passover was a pilgrimage feast. Many traveled from far and wide to get to Jerusalem. And the temple required burnt offerings in the form of cattle, sheep, and doves. And since local vendors knew that people would not travel such long distances with their own animals, vendors took advantage of the opportunity to turn the temple grounds into a veritable open-air flea market. "Get your fatted calf here." "Doves for sale. Buy two and get one free." "We've got sheep—one sheep for one denarius!"

What is more, the temple authorities levied a tax on all worshippers—a tax that could not be paid in Greek, Roman, or foreign coins. Thus like an international terminal in today's airport, money changers could set up shop and collect handsome fees for trading out currency.

It is safe to assume that such practices were not new. It is safe to assume that Jesus had witnessed such behavior before. Yet something was different this time. Jesus reacted in a way that was distinct and defiant. The Bible says that he began immediately driving out the vendors, turning over tables, and pouring out their coins while declaring, "You have turned my father's house into a marketplace."

I cannot help but to rehearse in my mind why this may have been the case. Maybe Jesus was tired of being an indifferent bystander. Maybe Jesus decided that he could no longer walk by the temple and act as if he didn't see the exploitation and abuse. Or maybe Jesus just reached his point where he, too, was "sick and tired of being sick and tired."

New Testament scholar and dean of Wake Forest Divinity School Gail O'Day asserts that what is instructive about this story is not simply Jesus's anger. Too many people, she contends, play up this point. But what she emphasizes in this story is Jesus's courage. In decrying against those who have turned his father's house into a marketplace, he isn't talking about simply the vendors. The vendors and moneychangers are just opportunistic cogs in an otherwise unjust machine. Jesus is calling out the power structure of the temple—those who have elevated their own thirst for power; those who have elevated their own lust for control; and those who have lifted their own greed over the concern of worshipping almighty God.

Thus at the busiest, most significant and most profitable feasts of the year, Jesus shuts down their self-serving operation. His actions awake people from their indifference and apathy. His actions call out power structures for their promotion of injustice. And, I want to suggest, his action shines light on what is the real sin of the vendors and temple authorities—their idolatry!

Idolatry—the worship of another god. Idolatry—that which becomes the object of our heart's desire. Idolatry—in the words of the sixteenth-century Reformer Martin Luther, "that which our hearts cling to and confide in."

This is why the lectionary links this narrative of Jesus at the temple with the Ten Commandments as set forth in the book of Exodus. For prior to God instructing the people to keep the Sabbath day, honor one's parents, never commit murder, steal, not bear false witness or covet what one's neighbor has, there is a clear and concise prohibition—you shall have no other gods before me! You will not make for yourself an idol, whether in the form of anything that is in heaven above, the earth beneath, or in water under the earth. You shall not bow down to worship anyone or anything else.

It seems that God realizes that if you and I get the first prohibition right, it will be a lot easier for us to adhere to the other prohibitions. But whenever we allow something to become the object of our faith; whenever we allow our hearts to cling and confide in something of our own creation, even if that thing is ourselves, then we will surely kill, steal, and destroy in its name.

The temple cult in Jerusalem ceased putting their trust and directing their devotion toward God. Their actions reveal a group who had begun to worship at the altar of their own security and status. This is why they did not find it difficult to exploit those who came to God's house to worship. This is why they did not find it difficult to take advantage of the sincere faith of those who came for the feast of the

Passover. For since they had replaced God with their own object of devotion, themselves, it was impossible for them to adhere to any of the other commandments.

If we are honest with ourselves, we do not have to look too far to see examples of this in our world. Consider the many false gods we worship. Too many of us worship the gods of money and material. Cash rules everything around us. And because cash is our king of kings and lord of lords, we allow it to dictate and determine our moral behaviors. It is a sin and a shame how many people have killed, stolen, deprived others of their rights in the name of profit or a financial bottom line.

This had to be one of the earliest lessons I learned as a child. Not in Sunday school, but in the backseat of my father's 1975 Oldsmobile. My dad thought he was so cool because he had a fancy new 8-track tape player installed. And he would play the O'Jays' album *Ship Ahoy* over and over again. And like it was yesterday I can still hear the lyrics:

> For the love of money, people will steal from
> their mother . . .
>
> For that lean, mean, mean green. Almighty
> dollar.

And if it's not the gods of money and material, it is the gods of position and power. As nations, as states, as institutions, as tribes, races, or religions, we use everything at our disposal to seek or secure our place at the top of the totem pole. This is what impelled the imperial West to enslave and colonize peoples throughout Asia and Africa. This is what catalyzes some to protest against equal opportunity for others. And this is what allows some to worship, in effect, their race, or their gender, or their ethnicity, or their heterosexuality.

For instance, it was the worship of one's "Germanness" that allowed some, like the couple in the movie *Judgment of Nuremberg*, to ignore the injustices directed against Jews in the mid-twentieth century; just as that same worship of "Germanness" allows some to ignore the severe Islamaphobia that is directed at the nearly four million Muslims living in Germany today.

Similar can be said of many Whites in Selma fifty years ago. Their faith, no matter how bad their material conditions, was put in the fact that they were born White. And it was this idolatry, worshipping of one's racial position that led to the injustices of Jim Crow and voter suppression in this nation. This is why when debating William Buckley in Cambridge in 1965, James Baldwin argued that the idol of race that consumed the White Southerner was in some ways much worse than what has happened to people of color there. "Something awful must have happened to a human being," Baldwin argued, "to be able to put a cattle prod against a woman's breasts. What happened to the woman is ghastly. What happens to the man who does it is in some ways much worse."

This is what I want us to remember during this Lenten season. Our posture of penitence should cause us to reflect on all of the gods that have commanded our attention and our devotion. Our posture of repentance should lead us to renounce all of the unjust behaviors that result from our commitment to these idols. And our posture of critical reflection should catalyze us to raise our voices against all of the structures of injustice that deny others the rights and opportunities that we tend to hoard for ourselves.

To the German couple who declared to Spencer Tracy, "we are just little people . . . Hitler created jobs. In terms of the Jews, we did not know about any of that. And if we did, what could we do?" It is clear that the idol of economic stability; an idol that Hitler held before them; it blinded them to the unjust treatment of the Jewish and so many others. It blinded them to their own loss—their loss of humanity due to their acceptance of the ordinariness of injustice.

But Jesus reveals to us this morning that one does not need much to stand up and be heard. Like those who answer the call to go to Selma, all we need is a voice of courage and a willingness to sacrifice our idols in order to love the Lord with all our hearts, and thus love our neighbors as ourselves.

Reverend Joseph Lowery, a respected lion of the civil rights movement, captures such a positive example. In 1982 he led a march from Alabama to Washington. The point of the march, in part, was to demand extension of the expiring section of the 1965 Voting Rights Act. The march began in Carrolton, Alabama, on a cold, wintry February day. Yet the SCLC received word that the local sheriff was delivering hams and turkeys to residents in order to dissuade them from attending the protest rally when they arrived in the next town. Lowery said that they made their way through a cold rain, and numbers were sparse. The entire time he was thinking, *I cannot believe the community abandoned us.* He could not believe that they would sacrifice their support for a truckload of hams and turkeys. Well, when Lowery and the few marchers completed the twelve-mile trek and approached the community center, they were greeted by a beautiful sight. There were hundreds of local residents gathered with their coats and marching shoes on. And they were holding baskets full of ham and turkey sandwiches.

I am here to say this morning that we can learn a lesson from these protesters. We can take all of the things we have—our money, our time, our educations, our power, privilege, and access—and rather than turning them into idols; rather than making them ends unto themselves; we can use all of these things to stand up for a beloved vision of God's kingdom. And when we do this, we will be able to lift our voices and sing with confidence:

> One day when the glory comes
>
> It will be ours, it will be ours
>
> One day when the war is won
>
> We will be sure, we will be here sure
>
> Glory, oh glory,
>
> Glory, glory, hallelujah, God's truth is marching on.

CST5: USE DIALECTICAL ARGUMENTATION TO INTERCONNECT CONTEMPORARY SITUATION AND BIBLICAL TEXT IN THE INTEREST OF HOMILETICAL EVENNESS.

Too many preachers shun prophetic preaching for fear of sounding too "political." The gospel isn't American politics, but to proclaim the gospel in time and space is unavoidably political, textually and rhetorically so. The scriptures do things with words as the preacher's words do things on the sacred imaginings of listeners. It is not gospel corruption when priority is given to seeing intertextual analogies in the biblical witness that speak to social injustice or when a certain *rhetorical situation* (combination of persons, events, or imperfection marked by urgency that invites the sermon's address) drives the preacher to sermon preparation instead of the biblical text driving the preacher's preparation. A preacher can be equally effective if the starting point is the situation or felt need of the congregation, and this is why when addressing a contemporary concern, pairing the right text with an isolated and clearly identifiable issue is critical. If wrongly paired, forced interpretation is inevitable and one's preaching will mute the gospel and become centered around a personal agenda. But when the text and situation are appropriately held in dialectical tension, injustice gets named and the listeners have something concrete to contemplate. In sum, they find new avenues for human engagement as the gathered and sent community of faith.

ENVIRONMENTAL WHOLENESS, MATERIALISM, AND SOCIAL RESPONSIBILITY

Few sermons on ecological justice and stewardship of the earth are heard from African American pulpits today.[5] But to recognize how self-serving behaviors breed social inequality and how the enthronement of unregulated consumerism in America has negative sociopolitical implications for environmental wellness, preachers are presented a homiletical obligation to prophetically challenge systems that keep the urban poor in poverty.

SERMONIC EXAMPLE ➡️

Sheila Ireland
"The Branding of Idolatry";[6] Daniel 3:1-18
African American Prophetic Preaching Course
Howard University School of Divinity
Washington, DC

Sheila Ireland's master's thesis "Urban Homiletics in Shades of Green"[7] seeks to address this public issue of ecological injustice. In a global society in which 62 percent of the world's population will reside in urban centers by 2050, she argues that one important way for the church to face the realities

---

5. For more resources on this subject, see Dianne Glave & Mark Stoll, *To Love the Wind and the Rain: African Americans and Environmental History* (Pittsburgh: University of Pittsburgh Press, 2005); Kimberly Smith, *African American Environmental Thought: Foundations* (Lawrence: University Press of Kansas, 2007); and Dianne Glave, *Rooted in the Earth: Reclaiming the African American Environmental Heritage* (Chicago: Chicago Review Press, 2010).

6. This sermon was delivered in my spring 2017 African American Prophetic Preaching course in which Sheila Ireland enrolled as a visiting consortium student.

7. Used by permission of Sheila Ireland. The sermon "The Branding of Idolatry" is one of ten sermons featured in her unpublished May 2017 master of arts in religion thesis titled "Urban Homiletics in Shades of Green" for Lutheran Theological Seminary at Gettysburg, Gettysburg, Pennsylvania.

of environmental decay and adapt to a highly urbanized climate is to build its "green preaching"—preaching themed based on commitments to environmental protection, care, and sustainability—portfolio.

In a sermon drawing on selected verses from the third chapter of the prophetic book of Daniel, Ireland demonstrates how a theo-centric (creator-centered) outlook that lifts up scripture's storied heroes—in this case the Hebrew boys Shadrach, Meshach, and Abednego—permits the preacher to critique culture. Worshipping Babylon's emperor is named as sin because to do so stands in opposition to God and God's sovereign care for God's own creation, namely, the socially marginalized in the urban environment. Without this sermon's clear-cut thematic focus, one might argue that the selected text and topic would be illogically paired. Forcing one's topic onto the text is often the result of illogical pairing.

SERMON BEGINNING

Healthcare providers, daycare providers, insurance providers, Internet service providers, training care providers, map providers, etc. It is my thinking, that some words should not be used to reference anything or anyone but God. Provider is such a word. Some words should be exclusive references to God because while people have a linguistic concept of the word, little thought is given to an antecedent or the history of its earlier life. Provider is such a word. Some words are germane to God only—because as it is written, in the beginning, God created . . . Provider is such a word. And some words are so discriminatively distinctive that they can only represent God. Provider is such a word, for every good and perfect gift comes from God. The first commandment from God is "You shall have no other gods before me."

The second is "You shall not make idols." God specifically told Moses to tell the Israelites, "Do not make any gods to be alongside me: do not make for yourselves gods of silver or gods of gold" (see Ex 20:23). In chapter 3 of the book of Daniel, God's first two commandments were faithfully obeyed by Shadrach, Meshach, and Abednego and grossly disobeyed by Nebuchadnezzar and the Babylonians. What can we learn from both responses? The chapter concludes with Shadrach, Meshach, and Abednego, serving as living examples of faith that also resulted in the modeling of an obedient, God-glorifying response to the oppression of being Hebrews living on the margins of Babylonian society. That is a lesson for the oppressed living on the margins of society today. What deep strategic plan did the Hebrew men employ? They obeyed God.

SERMON BODY

To be branded by idolatry leaves an irreverent stain of dependence on the idol that obscures our love and trust of God and estranges our relationship with God. That may be expected for Nebuchadnezzar and unbelievers whose greatest need is to know God. But the sinfulness of idolatry, the over-indulgence, inordinate admiration, love, and reverence for things apart from God to the point of reliance, is also common among believers. Nebuchadnezzar was branded by idolatry, as were the Babylonians in general. The problem with Nebuchadnezzar's idol is the problem with all idolatry, disobedience to God.

No worldly things, seen or unseen, are to come before God. When the Nebuchadnezzars of the world create an idol, you can be sure that, being a product of an idolater's human imagination, that idol will reflect human sin in general, and will most likely additionally reflect the discrete transgressions of its creator. No-thing should ever be placed ahead of God. In chapter 2, Daniel interpreted a dream for King Nebuchadnezzar, where God communicated an overview of world events. The king was the golden head on the statute in the dream. He was so impressed with the interpretation that he lavishly praised Daniel's God. Mere verses later in chapter three, Nebuchadnezzar, in sheer, idolatrous arrogance, set up a full-length, golden selfie, hoping to religiously unify the nation around it.

Nebuchadnezzar's identification with the statue is also apparent, when he questioned Shadrach, Meshach, and Abednego—again in sheer, idolatrous arrogance: "Who is the god who will deliver you out of the hands of my hands?" That is the language of the branding of idolatry.

Today, just listen for the preposition "after." God comes after. Example: I fully intend to serve God, after I accomplish my personal goals (that range from commodities to people), or after I finish partying. The human heart desires things that become substitutes for God. Nebuchadnezzar, overcome by idolatrous audacity, placed himself above the true and living God. His idolatry did what idolatry does. It changes the splendor of God into an image.

SERMON ENDING

That is what happens when one fraternizes with idols. The branding tool of reliance, in the hands of the golden statue created by Nebuchadnezzar, branded the king, "Dependent on me." Today, we are branded when we store up earthly provisions for selfish gratification. Our God of provision has demonstrated a godly model of care that stewards of the earth may follow by being people more interested in community well-being, than selfish idolatrous accumulation.

—CRAFTING STRATEGY: PREACHING ON THE PROPHETS—

Although, peculiarly enough, not much is known about the thought processes of the prophet, the Hebrew prophets' social world nonetheless has much to teach us about our social world. What can be stated without equivocation is that prophets did their work in environments of theological contestation.

CST1: CAPTURE A THEME FOR THE INTRODUCTION AND STICK WITH IT.

The sermon introduction might raise a question or explore illustratively the adverse effects of materialism, disease, greed, self-deception, intra-cultural violence, and poverty, all of which the Hebrew prophets' oracles have addressed (for other themes, see "Texts for Confronting Human Tragedy and Communal Despair" in chapter 3).

CST2: FIND AND SKETCH OUT HOW CHARACTERS IN PROPHETIC TEXTS DEPICT THE NATURE OF GOD'S INVOLVEMENT WITH HUMANKIND IN THE ANCIENT WORLD. BY DOING SO, THE PREACHER IS AFFORDED AN INTERPRETIVE WINDOW TO ADDRESS CONTEMPORARY SOCIAL CONCERNS BIBLICALLY.

As messengers of Yahweh, their primary task was to retrieve, announce, and interpret God's interventional acts within human communities. The contemporary preacher is likewise obligated to concretely name how God intervenes in today's world affairs. What social concerns might God expect us to address in a metaphoric valley of dried bones (e.g., *famine, communal death, land restoration, or climate change*)?

—CRAFTING STRATEGY: PREPARING THE SERMON BRIEF—

Every passage in the Bible has social, political, and theological implications. Preparing a sermon brief is a way to organize one's thinking around such implications. The task of writing a sermon brief serves at least three ends:

1. It helps preachers to become more conscientious of how their biblical and theological interpretation of Scripture affects the worldview of their congregational communities.

2. It promotes critical reflection on the task of sermon preparation as it helps preachers move from text to sermon, by relating their functional theology (i.e., their individual take on the Christian tradition and how these ideas might be integrated within his or her life and ministry) and convictions about God that lie at the heart of the text.

3. It urges preachers toward more thoughtful biblical exegesis and critical theological reflection on things that are happening in our contemporary social world.

CST1: PROBE PASSAGE AND WRESTLE OUT ITS MEANING-POTENTIAL.

After selecting the passage, reading and meditating on it, and paraphrasing the passage in your own words, now shift your mind to think like a researcher.

CST2: TEASE OUT ITS HISTORICAL, THEOLOGICAL, SOCIOCULTURAL, AND SOCIOPOLITICAL ELEMENTS.

Explore and engage the biblical text's historical, theological, sociocultural, and sociopolitical elements and relate them to some justice or ecclesial/pastoral care concern of our times. This work requires the use of good commentaries and other biblical resources. At the very least, I recommend reading commentary in study Bibles: *The Harper Collins Study Bible* (NRSV, fully revised and updated), *The Peoples Study Bible* (NRSV). Other helpful resources for exegesis are single book commentaries: *Abingdon New Testament Commentaries, Interpretation Commentary for Teaching and Preaching; Belief: A Theological Commentary*; multiple books volumes: *The New Interpreters Commentary, True to Our Native Land: New Testament Commentary, Paideia Commentaries on the New Testament, Baker Exegetical Commentary on the New Testament, Osborne New Testament Commentaries, Women's Bible Commentary*; lectionary commentaries: *Feasting on the Gospels Commentary, Feasting on the Word Commentary, Preaching God's Transforming Justice Commentary, Connections*

Commentary; online lectionaries—*African American Lectionary, Working Preacher.org*, reference books: *Harper's Bible Commentary, Harper's Bible Dictionary, The New Interpreters Bible: The New Testament Survey, The New Interpreters Bible: The Old Testament Survey, The Strong's Concordance, The Oxford Encyclopedia of the Bible and Arts* (many and more of these resources can be found using *LOGOS Bible* study software*).

THORNS AND THISTLES: HELPS NOT HANDCUFFS (PART 2)

There is always the understandable temptation to jump to the biblical and theological resources that sit well with your deeply cherished beliefs and convictions. My advice for you is to stretch yourself and broaden your scope academically and theologically. Why impoverish your exegetical imagination by chatting with your regular theological buddies every time you prepare a sermon? There's much fruit to be obtained from picking fights with commentators who have contrasting opinions on a subject or theme. Your consciousness gets nourished and strengthened when you seek to learn all points of view before preaching a sermon that addresses a public issue or ecclesial concern; and, this is especially important if you are handling highly controversial topics such as abortion and reproductive rights, homosexuality and same-sex unions/marriage, euthanasia, gun rights, war and militarism, nationalism and immigration, intimate partner violence and gender discrimination, judicial and legislative policies.

Consider the *Key Elements of Sermon Exegesis* as you craft your sermon brief.

1. Historical particulars—exploring the lifeworld of ancient writers and hearers by mining the history in/behind the text (pattern of events, archaeological details, date of composition, social setting, language, etc.).

2. Literary details—exploring the literary genre of the biblical text (history, laws, wisdom, prophecy, Gospels, epistles, apocalyptic, etc.) and, exploring the meaning of the passage based on responses to/from the biblical text as finished product (e.g., analysis of textual voice, meaning, movement, plot, structure, and social function).

3. Sociocultural relevance—wrestling out the text's meaning-potential relative to the interpreter's context-determined social location, existential experiences, and formative cultural tradition(s) (e.g., religious convictions, folkways, mores, that emanate from one's worldview).

4. Sociopolitical elements—noting how power is used in the text in relation to biblical characters, spiritual forces, and social systems (e.g., power dynamics in human conflicts in war or with other oppositional forces personal or spiritual).

The content of this sample brief shared below was written and first published in the lectionary volume *Preaching God's Transforming Justice: A Lectionary Commentary* (Abingdon), using its style guidelines. But here, as an example, I have expanded and reformatted it to be more accessible as a teaching tool for the reader.

THE SERMON BRIEF

The finished sermon brief need not be any longer than three to four pages double-spaced. Of course, if one is series preaching, you will want to extend page length. In preparing your brief, cite your sources.

Follow this outline:

Scripture text: Micah 6:1-8

v. 8 He has shown you, O mortal, what is good. And what does the Lord require of you? To act justly and to love mercy and to walk humbly with your God.

I. Opening paragraph—Begin with a one-line summary.

Micah reminds us to honor the grace of God by critiquing the status quo and struggling against unjust social arrangements.

II. Biblical commentary—Give an explanation of what is going on in this passage biblically.

The book of Micah is a policy critique. The book's main character, Micah of Moresheth, speaks the hard, divine word in the name of God. Forbearance for rebellious Israel no more! Micah is commissioned by God to scold his kinspeople. Israel's economic blessing under the reigns of Uzziah and Jotham secured their political clout in the region, but with her increased prosperity came "a strong current of egotistic materialism" that coincided with maltreatment of the poor by the ruling elite.[8] Preceding this sixth chapter, a verdict has been rendered: "I will execute vengeance on the disobedient." Israel's defiance against God's holiness code and failure to honor their fundamental obligation to practice justice is the marked offense. The political and religious gatekeepers ignored God's law and are therefore indicted for their wickedness.

"Thou shalt not covet," is one law clearly broken. The land of the field workers was coveted and seized, householders sustained injury by oppressive taxation under the religious watch of Jerusalem's prophets who cried out "peace," and the social elite lived undisturbed by the plight of the weak and poor (2:2; 3:5). The verdict "guilty" is merited by unrepentant Israel. In the sixth chapter, God challenges Israel. We are offered a stunning image of a divine magistrate exhausted of patience and fishing around for an admission of guilt from wayward Israel. Micah's biting oracle takes the tack of the parental reprimand, "Now what do you have to say for yourself?"

III. Sociocultural reflection—Give an example of how this text might relate to some aspect of our lived experience.

Although Emancipation had represented slavery's demise on paper, for Black sharecroppers, America's democratic experiment failed miserably. Exploited for their labor and swindled out of their rightful property by the unjust economic practices of their former slaveholders, they found themselves victims within an evil social system, similar to certain dwellers in the foothills of Judah.

---

8. Juan I. Alfaro, O.S.B., *Justice and Loyalty: A Commentary on the Book of Micah* (Grand Rapids: Eerdmans, 1989), 6.

IV. Sociopolitical or Pastoral Care commentary—Reflect on a public issue or pastoral care concern relative to your reading and engagement of the passage.

Sociopolitical

Unchecked authority may secure prosperity, but it carries with it the price tag of exploitation of the economically disenfranchised—the indigent human beings of society. This country's undocumented immigrant workers are hired to work in the suburbs and are paid menial wages to labor without guarantee of workers' rights. Who will plead the case for the undocumented person who performs tasks we would not? Who will work on the behalf of the residents in Flint, Michigan whose children have been exposed to high levels of lead contaminates found in Flint's water supply? Local and state government officials cut corners and put cost-saving ahead of the health and wellness of Flint's low-income residents, 60 percent of whom are African Americans.

Pastoral Care

In the end, the prophet Micah clearly sees that for Israel redemption will not come cheap. It will come at the cost of true religion and purity of heart. The avenue to redemption is good ethics and purity of heart. According to biblical scholar Juan Alfaro, "there is something worse than appearing before the Lord empty-handed . . . appearing before [the Lord] dirty-handed and empty-hearted, without justice."[9] To practice justice is to exercise compassion (loving mercy) for the poor and marginalized.

V. Theological commentary—What is God actively doing and saying in the text?

But one also hears the satiric chastisement of an exasperated Sovereign, "O my people, what have I done to you?" How have I failed you? Despite the rhetorical dance between a loving yet disappointed God and God's willful people, only one voice speaks with authority from the text. "Is this how you repay me after all I have done for you? I thought we had a deal?" To think about God's intimate feelings toward us is to perceive something about our own lives lived before a lovingly patient God. God says, "I have put the mountains and hills on the witness stand and they testify of your moral laxity

---

9. Ibid.

and abominable practices. The only requirement I have made of you is that you worship me wholeheartedly, 'to do justice, and to love kindness, and to walk humbly with me'" (vv. 3-8).

Brief summary

This passage gives witness to the justice and grace of God. To enthrone materialism over right worship and just practices is to break covenant with God.

→ **EXERCISE** ←

Select five prophets from the prophetic literature (e.g., Amos, Jeremiah, Ezekiel, Deborah, Daniel, Habakkuk, Huldah).

Explore the prophet's social scene, agenda, and prophetic book's content. Ask yourself where do ancient and contemporary horizons intersect and/or diverge? What continuities and discontinuities exist?

Create four columns and list details mindful of the prophet's social world (PRSW), the prophet's central concern (PRCC) in the passage, contemporary intersection (CI), and contemporary diversions (CD).

File away summaries to be drawn from at later times of sermon preparation.

Example:

PRSW (Prophet's Social World)

- Featured prophet—Amos

- Tekoa (home)

- Prophet of means (sheep herder and sycamore tree dresser)

- Native of Judah (the Southern Kingdom)

- Worked in Northern Kingdom between reigns of kings Uzziah and Jeroboam

- Served during relatively peaceful reigns

- The breakdown in old tribal and family systems yielded prosperity for a few wealthy families at the expense of the commoner

PRCC (Prophet's Central Concern)

- Merchants defrauded customers in marketplace (2:6)

- Religiously arrogant defamed worship (2:8; 5:21-24)

- Father and son commit morally reprehensible sexual acts (3:7)

- The wealthy and self-indulgent minority enjoyed and paraded their material excess (3:8; 6:4-7)

- Acts of bribery and dishonest governmental practices privilege few and disenfranchise others (5:11-12)

- The blatant disregard for and social abuse of the poor represented the spirit of the times (8:4)

CI (Contemporary Intersection)

- Prosperity gospel-centered worship practices are rooted in individualistic self-aggrandizement and often materially exploit and extort the poor

- Financial privileges are obtained by a wealthy few who benefit from taxation system and governmental policies

- The suffering poor are exploited by corporate entities that protect self-interest

- Dishonest capitalists benefit from exploitative lending and pay-to-play economic practices

- Criticism to empire-oriented systems and practices

CD (Contemporary Diversion)

- No theocratic political system of government

- No literal kingship or monarchial reigns

- Nations are representative of a different global region, outlook, and time period

- Burnt offerings and grain are incongruous with current religious giving practices

43

In pursuit of justice, *Exodus preaching unmasks systemic evil and opposes self-serving, deceptive human practices.* Sermons attentive to this mark use subversive rhetorical strategies aligned with the message and kingdom vision God enacted in the person of Jesus Christ. In the next chapter we turn our attention to the power of preaching *hope*, the second mark.

CONFRONTING HUMAN TRAGEDY AND COMMUNAL DESPAIR

We are in a mess. What are we going to do? We are witnessing the globalism of indifference.

—Cornel West[1]

Prophets were raised to speak truth to power, often in scolding ways. Though in most instances reluctant to assume their work, prophets acted as truth-telling mediators given the radical assignment of making public God's displeasure in religious apostasy and monarchial tyranny. This is well documented in the prophetic literature. Despite their prevailing charge to confront Israel and her foreign foes, Old Testament prophets also broadcasted visions and messages of hope.

In light of the prophets' task of coupling criticism and hope, by analogy, the preacher might discover creative ways of linking the New Testament witness of *the saving significance of Jesus's death as a liberative and redemptive vision* with the prophets' priestly role in the speech-act. Offering hopeful symbols to penetrate despair and to encourage the community to remain active and hopeful in the face of collective misery and societal neglect is prophetic criticism's essential counterpart. Jesus's anointed earthly life, atoning work on the cross, and victory over the grave is the substance of hope. His compassion "constitutes a radical form of criticism" because it takes suffering and death

---

1.   Quoted in a sermon at Andrew Rankin Memorial Chapel at Howard University on April 17, 2016.

seriously, and because hurt inflicted upon the marginalized is taken seriously, "hurt is not to be accepted as normal and natural but is [to be taken as an] abnormal and unacceptable condition for humanness."[2]

Exodus preaching remains interminably hopeful when confronted with human tragedy and communal despair.

Preaching from the New Testament should be refracted through the lens of Jesus's inaugural vision described in Luke 4:16-21. This text is not only the basis for the Christian preacher's discourse, it is the content of what makes preaching essential for the restoration of African American communities in particular and human communities in general. Self-referentially, in these verses Jesus recounts the prophet Isaiah's oracle to his hearers and presents himself as the embodiment of God's compassionate concern for humankind. To this Galilean community, Jesus declares that he is the one Israel has been anticipating. Put another way, in Jesus, messianic hope has arrived materially. An alternative to social decay and spiritual death has come in the person of Jesus Christ. Speaking Isaiah's words, as recorded in chapter 61, Jesus ushers in a not fully realized prophetic vision that summons human participation.

Although preaching practices are wide-ranging and extremely diverse in terms of arrangement, form, and modes and methods of delivery from setting to setting, Jesus's norm-setting vision for Christian proclamation captured in Jesus' words: "He has sent me to bring good news to the poor, proclaim release to the captives . . . recovery of sight to the blind, to let the oppressed go free," is the homiletical compass for prophetic preaching. This vision that Jesus declares he was anointed to set in motion, inviolably, must be seen as the ground floor upon which preaching stands or falls and the irreducible content of what preachers can and must speak. At the same time, this vision of the gospel handed on to us is neither reducible to human reasoning nor captive to any cultural landscape. Though God summons human participation, the prophetic word spoken is speech from God, about God, and that begins and ends with God.

---

2. Walter Brueggemann, *The Prophetic Imagination,* 2nd ed. (Minneapolis: Fortress, 2001), 88.

Without question similar challenges exist when preaching from the New Testament as they do from the Old Testament. Preaching from the Pauline epistles is indicative of this notion.

—CRAFTING STRATEGY: PREACHING FROM THE NEW TESTAMENT—

CST 1: RETHINK YOUR APPROPRIATION AND PRIORITIZATION OF PAUL.

Too often preachers make christological claims that are doctrinally faithful but gospel deficient. This may seem contradictory, but the truth is, much of our homiletical thinking as interpreters of scripture owes greater intellectual debts to the Protestant Reformers of the sixteenth century than to the testimony of the unlettered scholars who walked with Jesus. Nancy Lammers Gross convincingly argues that when we preach Paul "we tend to preach the Reformers' interpretation of Paul" based on what Paul said, which may be attached to an agenda not related to the intention of biblical text.[3] The carryover from the Reformers' formula that found homiletical embrace manifested in four ways: (1) preachers began to preach Paul as if his authorial aim was to present the world a systematic theology; (2) preachers used his letters as a proof text or launching pad to serve a particular sermonic agenda; (3) preachers reduced Pauline passages to a kernel of truth; and (4) preachers preached Paul syllogistically through linear, rational deductive argument.

Instead of preaching the message of the cross carrying the Reformers' preaching methodology to the pulpit Sunday to Sunday, a more faithful approach, Lammers Gross maintains, is to preach Paul using stereoscopic imagination, that is, "to preach the word of the cross in ways consistent with its apocalyptic context and content . . . [versus] merely explaining Paul's words about the cross."[4]

Given that thirteen books of the New Testament are ascribed to Paul, dismissing Pauline thought outright will simply not do. Still, seldom are the theological claims of pivotal icons of the Christian tradition challenged by working preachers today. In my view, the Reformers and the apostle Paul for that matter, despite their herculean theological contributions to profligate, defend, and clarify the doctrinal tenets of the Christian faith, must be regarded, like

---

3. Nancy Lammers Gross, *If You Cannot Preach Like Paul* (Grand Rapids: Eerdmans, 2002), 17.

4. Ibid, 19.

we ourselves, as secondhand interpreters of the earthly ministry, death, burial, and resurrection of Jesus Christ.

When preachers fail to take into account that all theology, past and present, is provisional, or fail to acknowledge that the culture we grow up in shapes the way we interpret the world and the texts we handle, the real message communicated is that God's revelation is era-captured and that we who preach the gospel are culturally bleached passive players having little new to say about God's unfolding revelation for Christian living. If our personal encounters with a living God are just that, ours and personal, then our religious landscapes and the rhetorical situations that summon our participation in delivering the gospel must be seen as equal in significance to those of Paul's world. As not to relativize Paul, however, a counter proposition should be noted. Some scholars have argued that in proclaiming the gospel to non-Jewish audiences Paul was in effect preaching subversively in opposition to empire. And so Paul does not engage directly in political action to change the status quo, not because he favors it but because he thinks that the end of time has commenced and very soon, in his lifetime, Jesus Christ will come to establish a new order, the kingdom of God. In light of this, the preacher does well not to dispose of the Pauline corpus but rather to interpret it emphasizing Paul's use of the kingdom of God as an eschatological ideal and norm, that is, as optimism about social and historical change leading inevitably to God's kingdom—and this coming kingdom as the standard by which to evaluate present social structures.

CST2: RESPECT THE JEWISHNESS OF JESUS IN LIGHT OF PAUL'S CITIZENSHIP PRIVILEGE.

In his now-classic book *Jesus and the Disinherited* theologian and mystic Howard Thurman replays a scene of a conversation he had with his illiterate grandmother, who would frequently request he read the Bible to her. She especially loved hearing the Psalms. However, because White ministers would load up their sermons with texts such as "slaves, be obedient to your masters" (Eph 6:5-8) she prohibited Thurman from reading any of Paul's letters to her. Thurman's grandmother was hermeneutically astute enough to notice the incompatibility of this Pauline imperative with the liberating message of the gospel of Jesus. According to Thurman, it was this repeated exchange with his grandmother that prompted him into deeper investigation into Paul.

After probing, Thurman came to the conclusion that if one solely interprets Christ's meaning through the lens of atonement, it is likely that Jesus's social position as a disinherited Palestinian Jew will be overlooked. And while Thurman's overarching goal is more specific as he sets up an analogous picture of the disinherited Jews of Jesus's day and America's disinherited masses of Blacks and oppressed others, his demonstration of why texts must be interpreted through the filters of power and social privilege is instructive for preachers. Juxtaposing Jesus's biography and Paul's, Thurman lays out the following facts:

- Jesus was a Jew just as Paul was a Jew.

- Paul was the first great interpreter of Christianity.

- Paul penned letters older than the Gospels themselves.

- Because Paul was not of the original twelve, his full-fledged authority to speak on Jesus was met with suspicion by early church leaders.

- Though alike in Jewishness, Paul, unlike Jesus, was a free Jew and a Roman citizen.

- Paul belonged to a privileged class, which meant he could directly appeal to Caesar, and thus could claim rights that neither Jesus nor his disciples ever enjoyed.[5]

In view of these facts, it is not a stretch to see that Paul's sense of social security would influence certain aspects of his interpretation of the Christian faith. Though refusing to boast, Paul was not a disinterested interpreter.

Because Paul had the guaranteed protections of the state, he undoubtedly had some regard for the stability of his own social position. In Paul's social world, argues Thurman, one should hardly be surprised that Paul would be comfortable saying, "Slaves, obey your masters." Biblical texts are weighted with sociopolitical meaning; exploring how power is used and by whose hands power is being used in specific passages must always be on the preacher's exegetical radar. By this illustration, Thurman is simply suggesting that social privilege equates to power of access and with access comes the human proclivity to protect those who protect us. Or, as Thurman puts it, "unless one actually lives day by day without a sense of security one cannot properly understand what worlds separated Jesus from Paul at this point."[6]

As significant as Paul is to our understanding of the Christian faith, the theologically attentive preacher who would preach cross-resurrection in a prophetic mode will not overlook the sociopolitical elements and power dynamics that are always in play when interpreting texts. Protecting systems that support the freedom for some invariably equates to obstructing paths to freedom for others.

---

5. Howard Thurman, *Jesus and the Disinherited* (Boston: Beacon, 1996), 21–23.

6. Ibid., 23.

Another consideration for readers who over-privilege Paul is that one explores passages in the Gospels, such as Luke's record of the conversion of Zaccheus/Levi and the call of the disciples. References to faith and believing in Luke are not set dogmatically as doctrinal teaching to be embraced, but rather, people practice trust and commitment by leaving everything behind to follow Jesus. In other words, their faith is realized in their faithfulness (Luke 19:1-10; 23:39-43).

Homiletician Sally Brown maintains that our job as preachers is not to explain, for example, the meaning of "atonement in terms of comprehensive abstraction" but to help persons imagine redemption in particular, concrete situations. While she is not implying that atonement theories (metaphors and models) have a diminished role in understanding humanity's redemption, this means that preaching will:

- be more pastoral than theoretical in terms of its character;

- be more evocative than comprehensive in its aims;

- be more textured by exploration (interpreting the cross in new imaginative ways) rather than seeking closure and completeness.

PREACHING LIFE-CROSS-RESURRECTION IN A DEATHLY WORLD

What we do in the pulpit is theology, and theology in the broadest sense is speaking of a promise-bearing God who redeems and speaks to the real needs of real people. Because theology is practiced in community (public), part of that particular community's story ought to be apparent in the preacher's proclamation. Black preaching must reclaim this if it is to speak to the listener's lived experience and existential situation. It is not enough to speak about redemption in an objective sense that leaves us in the world of the biblical text; to speak about the cross truthfully and persuasively is to be drawn into its image of vulnerability and come face to face with a God undergoing death to defeat all that is deadly. Preaching about the cross, as Sally Brown puts it, is a twofold task that is both critical and constructive. The first task is to clear away false understandings, and the second is to help congregations find faithful ways of "reimagining redemption."[7]

---

7.   Sally A. Brown, *Cross Talk: Preaching Redemption Here and Now* (Louisville: Westminster John Knox, 2008), 26–28.

To see this fully is to discover that preaching holds together in a trinitarian pattern: life-cross-resurrection (living, lamentation, and celebration). To focus on any one or two aspects exclusively is to miss the way of Christ.

SERMONIC EXAMPLE ➡

Howard-John Wesley
"When the Verdict Hurts"; Mark 15[8]
Alfred Street Baptist Church
Alexandria, VA
2013

News of the tragic gun death of Trayvon Benjamin Martin, a seventeen-year-old African American youth, on the night of February 26, 2012, in Sanford, Florida, at the hands of shooter George Zimmerman, a biracial White and Hispanic neighborhood watch coordinator, began receiving widespread attention a month later after hundreds of students from his high school in north Miami-Dade County, Florida, staged a walkout in support of Trayvon. With the help of social media, what began in local protest quickly became a national campaign against racial profiling and a call to repeal Florida's "Stand Your Ground" gun law. On April 5, 2013, Martin's parents settled a wrongful-death suit against the Twins Lakes gated community, but when George Zimmerman waived his right to a pretrial immunity hearing later that April, Zimmerman's attorneys decided they would try this as a self-defense case.[9] In the groundswell of mass rallies and protest demonstrations across the country, the trial began on June 24, 2013, after the six-member, all-female (with only

8. Live recording transcript. Sermon was delivered extemporaneously before a "talk-back" gathering on July 14, 2013, at the 11 a.m. service at the Alfred Street Baptist Church in Alexandria, Virginia, where Howard-John Wesley serves as senior pastor. Howard-John Wesley, "When the Verdict Hurts," live recording, YouTube video, 27:57, posted by "AlfredStreetHD," July 15, 2013, https://youtu.be/hqhOe85_vA8.

9. "Trayvon Martin Shooting Fast Facts," CNN Library, http://www.cnn.com/2013/06/05/us/trayvon-martin-shooting-fast-facts/, updated 1:47 p.m. on February, 22, 2014. As of the time of this writing, several other high-profile events have occurred regarding the crisis issue of shooting deaths of unarmed young African American men and women. Two include the killing death of seventeen-year-old Black teen Jordan Davis by Michael Dunn, a White citizen in Jacksonville, Florida, on November 23, 2012, and the fatal shooting death of eighteen-year-old Black teen Michael Brown by Darren Wilson, a White police officer in Ferguson, Illinois, on August 9, 2014, which sparked intense debate regarding violence and Black and White relations in the United States. Arguments have centered on racial profiling, but also on the question about whether undue attention is given to the deaths of Black boys at the hands of Whites instead of a heightened focus on Black-on-Black shooting violence.

one non-White) jury was selected. Jurors had three choices: to find Zimmer-man guilty of second-degree murder; to find him guilty of the lesser charge of manslaughter; or to find him not guilty. On Saturday, July 13, the verdict was read and George Zimmerman was found not guilty.

In the immediate aftermath of the jury's verdict, following an early morning conference call with a cadre of young African American clergy from across the country, Reverend Dr. Howard-John Wesley ascended the historic Alfred Street Baptist Church pulpit to address his five-thousand-member congregation with a message titled "When the Verdict Hurts." The opening line of *Time* magazine's religion writer Elizabeth Dias's article on Howard-John Wesley's sermon reads: "If you hear one sermon about America's Trayvon Martin moment, let it be this one."[10] Wesley, the not-yet-forty, eighth pastor in the church's 211-year history, is the father of two sons, both of whom are mentioned in this stirring sermon.

SERMON FRAGMENT

> I was on a phone call this morning with pastors who were praying together and preparing what they were going to speak in this moment. Dr. Otis Moss, who I will be with this weekend in revival, said that his heart hurt because his son came to him and asked him, "Daddy, am I next?" So I hurt. But not only do I hurt, I am confused. I am confused because how in the world a young Black man's life can be taken and the one who killed him can walk away with a handshake and a smile? I am not a lawyer. I don't seek to understand the complexities between homicide, murder, and manslaughter. I know this, "A young Black boy is dead. And nobody is paying the price for it." And I am confused legally. And I am also confused theologically. Don't act like your Bible is so big and you understand it so well. That at times you don't wrestle with what God seemingly allows to go down that doesn't make any sense . . . confused theologically about how to find and place God in the midst of a verdict like this. On that phone call we were speaking about this this morning, one of my good friends, the Rev. Dr. Nathan Scovins, said that he was confused because his son came to him and asked him, "Daddy, is George Zimmerman going to heaven?"
>
> I know what my Christian answer is supposed to be, and I know that don't bother you because you are saved, sanctified, and filled with

---

10. Elizabeth Dias, "The Best Sermon about Trayvon That You Will Hear: Pastor Howard-John Wesley Rallies His Congregation to Push Back against the Verdict," *Time Magazine,* July 18, 2013, http://swampland.time.com/2013/07/18/the-best-sermon-about-trayvon-that-you-will-hear/.

the Holy Ghost. But sometimes answering a question like that in a moment like this is a lot harder than Sunday school prepared you for. I'm hurt and confused, and Derrick, "I'm disappointed. I'm disappointed in that verdict. But Faye, I'm not surprised. I don't believe I am the only one who saw this coming." When this man wasn't even arrested until weeks after the slaying . . . something said that he was going to walk away. It's not even about the "Stand Your Ground" law. It's not even about if the prosecution was too aggressive in seeking second-degree murder instead of manslaughter. I saw this coming and you know this is the difficult thing and why you put me up to this mic to say what you're thinking, that I have a racial consciousness that lets me know that in situations like this, it typically doesn't work out in our favor. And, I know you can't say this and be politically correct and bring it up at your job because they will send you to HR, but I can say it in this place. What would be the outcome if the color roles were reversed? If this were a young Black man taking a White person's life, would we be wrestling with this this morning? There's a racial consciousness about this that really, if I can be honest with you, angers me. I want to take race out of it. I want to live in a world were I'm not judged by the color of my skin but by the content of my character. I want to live in a world where we are all created and treated equally. I want to live in a world where we are not separate but equal, but we are unified regardless of race and creed. But the reality is that I have to look at this through the eyes of a Black man.

With Paula Deen, the Supreme Court ruling, and now this, there's a racial consciousness that rises up within me that somehow taints my ability to see this objectively. I'm angry. How in the world can Michael Vick go to jail for two years for taking the life of an animal and a man kill a Black boy and walk away scot-free? I know that's not the button I should be pushing. But it sends a sign that the life of an animal is more protected than the life of our Black and Brown children. And, I struggle with this. The Rev. Doctor doesn't but the Howard-John does. Wondering what do you do when a verdict comes down that hurts like this. And the Lord reminded me that this is not the first time we've had to learn to live with a verdict that hurts. Come on out of 2013 and journey back to antiquity in Jerusalem with me and allow me to show you another travesty of justice.

After taking his text from Mark 15:21, which reads: "They compelled a passer-by, who was coming in from the country, to carry [Jesus's] cross; it was Simon of Cyrene, the father of Alexander and Rufus," an impassioned, at times tearful Wesley continues in his note-free delivery:

> I want to ask you to give me a little bit of time to take off the Reverend Doctor, Pastor and put on the Howard-John for a moment and tell you as I stand here like many of you. I come here with a mixed bag of emotions. In one way, I am hurt. I hurt with Trayvon's mother and father. To receive the double blow of not only losing their son but also now realizing that there may be no justice for his death. I hurt because Trayvon Martin reminds me of my own sons and how fragile Black life really is. I hurt because there are almost fifty Black lives taken by other Black hands in my own hometown of Chicago just last weekend.[11]

Then reflecting over a phone conversation he had with pastors preparing to preach that morning, Wesley replays the conversation he had had with his pastor friend and colleague Dr. Otis Moss III, who reported to him that he too was hurting, especially after Moss's son came to him and asked, "Daddy, am I next?"[12]

This front matter gets all the more personal as he continues to process the community's grief and disappointment with the legal process.

> I am confused because how in the world a young man's life can be taken and the one who killed him can walk away with a handshake and a smile? I am not a lawyer. I don't understand the complexities between homicide, murder, and manslaughter. I know this. A young Black boy is dead. And nobody is paying the price for it.[13]

Wesley looks to the text for succor. He works as a homiletical typologist and reminds his congregation that unjust verdicts are not new to people who have dealt with oppression and injustice. He says, "The Lord reminded me that this is not the first time we've had to live with a verdict that hurts. Come out of 2013 and journey back to antiquity in Jerusalem with me and allow me to show you another travesty of justice."[14] He describes it in this way:

11. Wesley, "When the Verdict Hurts."
12. Ibid.
13. Ibid.
14. Ibid.

A brother is on trial. Some of ya'll don't know him. His name is Jesus. And he's brought up on some charges that have no validity. He's accused of being subversive to the Roman government, of encouraging citizens not to pay taxes, and of calling himself a king. And there's a weak judge on the bench who represents the oppressive Roman government by the name of Pilate. And Pilate looks at the evidence and knows it is all circumstantial. He knows it's all hearsay . . . that there's no bonafide evidence that Jesus is guilty, and Pilate wants to dismiss the case not once but twice.[15]

In the sense that Trayvon's case is mismanaged and death is the consequence, Wesley seemingly suggests that Trayvon becomes a type of Christ. But the preacher is careful not to press this analogy too far. He imaginatively reconstructs the ancient picture. Jesus makes his way to Calvary, and his portrait of agony is particularly gruesome and unique.

Our Savior who has been beaten within a breath of his life, bloodied, and bruised, severely dehydrated, is weak and is yet called to carry a wooden beam that weighs at least one hundred pounds. He's carrying it through the streets of Jerusalem and his humanity kicks in. He's weak. He's dehydrated. He's bloodied and bruised. And he stumbles and falls. The Romans say the crucifixion has got to keep going. Got to get going to Calvary. The Bible says that there is a brother on the side of the street whose name is Simon.[16]

For effect, Wesley's hermeneutical strategy crafts a biblical portrait that ties together theology and cultural imagery. Casting Jesus and Simon as Black retrieves James Cone's metaphoric interpretation of a God who is ontologically Black and identifies with the existential realities of oppressed people. And Simon is pressed into the service of the preacher's illustrative proclamation. Simon is compelled to carry the cross. Wesley humanizes Simon, develops his character in the drama, and declares, analogously, that his listeners are twenty-first-century Simons forced to bear the weight of living with a mangled judicial process.

Now I need you not to misinterpret that term *compel*. He did not do it of his own volition. That word *compel* is a euphemistic way of

---

15.　Ibid.

16.　Ibid

saying that the same Roman government who found Jesus guilty, even though he was innocent, are now the soldiers who forced Simon to carry the weight of a cross that is the result of an unjust verdict. Make sure you hear this. Here is a brother who now has to bear a weight that is the result of an unjust verdict. He has no choice in the matter. He cannot escape it. The reality is . . . he's got to learn to carry that weight. Good morning, "Simon" . . . because that's what you have to learn to do today. To carry the weight that comes as a result of an unjust verdict. And we are compelled to do it. Not because we want to, but because it's done and double jeopardy exists and Zimmerman is innocent. And you've got to bear the weight of the bitterness it leaves in your soul.[17]

Wesley follows with a relevant question that drives the sermon to its gospel resolution. "How does this brother [Simon] carry the weight?" And by inference, how must we? Wesley proposes three calculated actions. First, because he is an African and in Jerusalem at Passover time, a season of reflective contemplation, Wesley posits that Simon finds strength in memory—"remembering where the Lord has brought him from . . . that is where we find strength to bear this weight."[18] With embroidered speech, he continues, calling the roll:

Because if anybody ought to remember what the Lord has done, it ought to be those who have some genes in Africa. Those who know the Lord has brought us up out of Africa . . . carried us through slavery and brought us to where we are right now. We have dealt with this before! He carried us through Emmitt Till! He carried us through the 16th Street Baptist Church in Birmingham, Alabama! He carried us through James Byrd and Yusuf Hawkins! He carried us through Rodney King! And God will carry us through this![19]

Second, says Wesley,

He bears this weight because he is the father of Rufus and Alexander. He carries this weight because his boys are with him [a creative exegetical leap, not literally stated in Mark's record, but used to good rhetorical effect]. And if he doesn't carry this weight, the penalty may

---

17. Ibid

18. Ibid

19. Ibid

rest upon his sons. He's the father of Rufus and Alexander. Put your children's names there. And he says, "I've got to carry this weight so that they don't have to."[20]

Later on in the sermon, he recalls the name Rufus and situates him as one of the leaders Paul mentions in his letter to the Roman church.

Paul begins to commend the leaders of the church in Rome, and when he gets to the end, he says, "and don't forget to hug Rufus." The young boy who watches his father carry the weight is a young boy who winds up in Rome . . . proclaiming the good news of Jesus Christ. The same young boy who watched his daddy bear the weight is the young man that grew up and stood in the middle of the same city and declared, "Jesus is Lord."[21]

As a responsible postmodern preacher-exegete, Wesley takes a race-conscious approach to the sermon, but publicly states that it is important how one responds to injustice. Wesley states:

We have to carry this weight correctly because we've got some Rufuses and Alexanders who are watching how we respond to this . . . I don't want to carry this incorrectly because I have a Cooper and a Deuce [names of his sons]. And I don't want them to grow up and use a bitterness of racial injustice to cause them to be unproductive in the world because they blame race on everything.

We've got to carry it correctly so that our sons and daughters will know that regardless of the color of their skin that God has given them the strength to be productive . . . that they can stand in the midst of an unjust world and continue to raise their voice in the name of Jesus. And the Lord will give them strength. We must not riot. We must not become hateful. We must not become bitter. We must bear this weight with the dignity of our forefathers and foremothers, so that our children can be productive.[22]

In a final word, he drives home his third point. He notes that while Simon carried the cross, Jesus walked in front of him. The vivid picture is

---

20. Ibid
21. Ibid
22. Ibid

painted for his listeners. Wesley concludes that Simon was able to carry the cross because he kept his focus on Jesus.

CST3: KNOW THAT LISTENING TO THE MEDIA AND COMMENTARY SPIN IS A TWO-EDGED SWORD.

The preacher has to be in touch with what her or his Sunday hearers imbibe from various electronic or paper outlets. A preacher who gets messages doctrinally sound but disregards the goings on in the public square will not meet the people where they are and will not appropriately discern the itch that requires the appropriate scratch.

CST4: JETTISON THE INTENDED SCRIPT TO ADDRESS BREAKING NEWS AND CORPORATE CONCERNS.

The preacher makes covenant with God but is always accountable to the charge of loving the people of the congregation who acknowledged the preacher's call as one set apart to feed the flock. Parishioners arrive at church with all sorts of commentary running through their minds after a week of social networking, hearing the breaking news of the day, witnessing protests because some gross injustice has occurred and brought injury upon a select group of people, and after watching a high dose of televangelism without regard to whether it coheres with the local minister's theology. In most historically Black worship settings, if there's some highly publicized tragedy, local or national, the preacher is expected to at least call the matter to the congregation's attention. Though preachers can't reconfigure their homiletical assignments each week, the preacher who ignores tragic events or brushes them under the carpet, will often be thought of as closed off from the chaotic and deathly world parishioners live in from Sunday to Sunday.

ADVOCATING FOR NEGLECTED AND ENDANGERED YOUTH

A preacher who is not moved by the burdens people carry should not expect to do much for God. When speaking on behalf of the voiceless the preacher should not forsake the task of probing root causes that render children or the elderly vulnerable in society. To what extent does the church contribute to the cycle of neglect? Does neglect stem from systemic concern that the preacher can name concretely and localize regarding its effects on a particular group of people? Take, for example, the lead poisoning of children in Flint, Michigan, that reached the level of crisis due to governmental neglect and malfeasance but could have been mitigated if persons in power had not cut corners. What factors contributed to decisions to ignore the crisis to the extent that it was ignored? What will be the long-term strain on the community? Are there indicators that the preacher can concretely identify that would suggest that the lead poisoning crisis will have enduring effects? What does this do to the economy of Flint? Was the community in dire straits prior to public outcry?

The issue of educational disparity has direct effects on the thriving of Black youths. What behavior challenge must the preacher render to families or to churches that make little room for discussion? In a sermon about youth endangerment, what are five concrete actions that can be named to rally the community to address the concern?

TEXTS FOR CONFRONTING HUMAN TRAGEDY AND COMMUNAL DESPAIR

Below are scriptural passages and themes drawn from the whole counsel of scripture for anchoring one's preaching and teaching throughout the course of the year. Consider these conspicuous themes that can be extracted from these passages as you prepare the gospel sermon (note the movement from form of injustice to hopeful response or remedy).

Genesis 21:9-21 (*Hagar and Ishmael*—abandonment, social dominance, helplessness, and promise)

Exodus 8:1; 23:9-12 (*Egyptian Bondage*—alienation, courage, oppression, and vindication)

Deuteronomy 10:17-22 (*The Law*—sovereignty, strength, justice, love, and provision)

Nehemiah 5:1-13 (*Building during Famine*—lack, sacrifice, indebtedness, servitude, intra-cultural violence, and restoration)

Job 24:1-12; 40–42 (*Complaints of Violence*—uprooting land-marks, property seizure, theft, physical abuse, humility, and satisfaction)

Psalms 22; 23; 37; 73; 82; 91; 103:1-6 (*Lament and Celebration*—suffering, hostility, emotional distress, trouble, wickedness, trust, patience, protection, provision, mercy, goodness, vindication, and salvation)

Isaiah 40:25-31; 55:1-9 (*Concern in Distress*—neglect, idolatry, penalty, death, exhaustion, power, strength, and renewal)

Jeremiah 33:1-11 (*Punishment and Guilt*—death, battle, sin, wickedness, abundance, healing, recovery)

Ezekiel 34:20-26 (*False Prophets*—greed, deception, unac-countability, apathy, social neglect, judgment, salvation, peace, covenant-keeping, and blessing)

Micah 4:1-4 (*Security and War*—wicked rulers, lamentation, in-struction, fellowship, peace, stability, and prosperity)

Habakkuk 2:1-5; 3:17-19 (*Complaint and Woe*—violence, sur-veillance, pride, arrogance, foreign threat, spiritual vision, and righteousness)

Matthew 5:1-11; 25:31-46 (*The Beatitudes*—poverty, mourning, persecution, kingdom access, comfort, spiritual satiation, heir-ship, and promised reward)

Mark 8:1-9 (*The Famished Multitude*—hunger, lack, overpopula-tion, economically underserved, compassion, obedience, sharing, and plenty)

Luke 4:16-21; 5:12-16, 17-26; 7:18-30 (*Anointing, Healing, Discipling*—poverty, spiritual captivity, rejection, disease, infir-mity, evil spirits, condemnation, doubt, disbelief, salvation, good news for oppressed, healing, forgiveness, and cleansing)

John 5:1-18; 6:1-15 (*Reimaging the Sabbath*—blindness, paraly-zation, suffering, sickness, legalism, condemnation, murder, hun-ger, lack, healing, miracle, obedience, grace, and power)

Romans 8:18-28; 12:9-21 (*Future Hope and True Discipleship*—spiritual slavery, orphaning, communal suffering, bondage, pain, freedom, mourning, heirship, adoption, love, affection, and goodness)

Galatians 6:1-10 (*Burden Sharing*—transgression, temptation, self-deceit, deception, weariness, goodness, sharing, empathy, co-operation, reaping, and sowing)

Hebrews 6:10-20 (*Despair and Faith Abandonment*—death, disobedience, contempt, curse, perfection, resurrection, spiritual gifts, and harvest)

James 2:1-10 (*Human Inequality*—greed, parading wealth, favoritism, poverty, evil thoughts, social dishonor, gross materialism, sin, love of neighbor, and accountability)

1 Peter 5:1-11 (*Communal Care*—social neglect, intergenerational division and strife, pride, anxiety, devil as devouring presence, glory, humility, exhaltation, steadfastness, and faith)

1 John 4:7-21 (*False Prophecy and Spiritual Discernment*—deception, lies, antichrist, worldliness, entrapment, faith confession, error, awareness, sovereignty, and truth)

Revelation 7:9-17 (*God's Righteous Reign and Eschatalogical Vision*—hunger, thirst, death, mourning, fellowship, diversity, salvation, power, blessing, glory, shelter, guidance, and comfort)

SERMONIC EXAMPLE

Toni Belin Ingram
"Fishing, Feeding, Tending, Following, Fish, Sheep and Lambs"; John 21:16-17
Canon Chapel, Emory University
Atlanta, GA
2013[23]

Reverend Toni Belin Ingram, upon receiving her master of divinity from Emory's Candler School of Theology in 2007, was ordained an itinerant elder in the AME Church and appointed in 2008 to lead Greater Smith Chapel AME in the Kirkwood section of Atlanta, Georgia, becoming the first woman to pastor the congregation. Belin Ingram was born into a family of pastors and church leaders. The daughter of an AME bishop, she has brought to her pastoral charge a passion for preaching and core commitments to fashioning a

---

23. Original manuscript of a sermon delivered at Emory University's Canon Chapel, Candler School of Theology, on April 9, 2013.

congregational ministry that embraces traditional Christian values while utilizing contemporary methods. The church's motto, "A Place Where Everyone Is Welcome," is reinforced by Ingram's openness to both churched and unchurched populations who attend worship services at Greater Smith Chapel.

With specific programs targeting young people, her congregation has reestablished its role as one of Kirkwood's leading institutions providing spiritual nurture, social services, and political change for the community. While the church is small in membership size, she has set up initiatives that provide free meals for youth during the summer, free tutoring services throughout the school year, and financial literacy education in hopes to eradicate cycles of poverty within Black households. Not unlike many predominately Black neighborhoods in Greater Atlanta, the communities around Greater Smith Chapel are undergoing gentrification. Despite this, Belin Ingram's active involvement in Kirkwood area schools and her service on community boards helps her to keep the needs of her congregation at the forefront.

Although the featured sermon was not preached before her local congregation, her core commitment to prophetic ministry in spoken Word is captured in her sermon delivered in April 2013 for a children's Sabbath worship service at her Methodist-affiliated alma mater, Candler Theological Seminary.

In this somewhat awkwardly titled sermon based on a reading in John's Gospel, Belin Ingram reminds her educationally privileged listeners that the vocation to which they have been called requires servant leadership. As she invites the Canon Chapel congregation of teachers and seminarians to assess carefully whether or not they are truly practicing what they preach and teach, she exposes the self-deceptive practices of busyness as a force that blinds ministers to their missional obligation to confront human tragedy and community neglect. She begins, "Fishing, tending, feeding, following, fish, lamb and sheep, what does that matter here? Do you ever think, 'I am too busy with my theological studies that I really have no time to be bothered to practice what I "preach" or "teach" [and that] . . . the Lord understands why I am too busy to do anything but this work that God Godself has ordained to my hands'?"

She then turns to the passage and extracts the central idea of the sermon. From the passage, Belin Ingram infers that love of God necessitates loving and serving people. In Jesus's instruction to Peter to feed and tend his sheep (serve and disciple believers), contemporaries also must make this ultimate priority in their ministries. Compassion provides foundation for a ministry that matters, she explains. Elements of the prophetic paradigm emerge in the following excerpt in the main body of the sermon as she connects the theme of service to a focus on youth and the myriad challenges they are facing. She maintains that the endangerment of youth is so widespread and overwhelming that the church's capacity as first responders has severely weakened. She asserts,

> When you look out and see what's happening on the news where kids are shooting one another, selling drugs to each other, and girls and boys are being exploited sexually . . . legislation is being written to take away services as opposed to securing more services. Education in low-income areas tends not to be as serious an undertaking as in the more affluent parts of town.
>
> When you look out and see children being split from their families because our immigration laws suck, and even in such a progressive time, we still have way too many babies having babies. There is so much going on from children living in poverty to those living with HIV/AIDS, to those with little or no healthcare . . .
>
> What about the Amber alerts that are now coming across our phones, kids living on the street and in tent cities, children who can't learn when they get to school because their basic need of food hasn't been met, children who come to school dirty and those who are clean but wearing last year's clothes and shoes that no longer fit, kids who have everything at their fingertips but no love . . .

In these crucial segments of the sermon, the preacher names multiple exigencies that strangle the lifeblood of children, especially those who reside in poor communities. Belin Ingram names the reality of child suffering and advocates for them. She keeps her message simple and subversive, the astonishing revelation in educating her non-impoverished listeners who undoubtedly hold differing theological positions on what justice entails and demands. The excerpts show her astute knowledge of the rhetorical situation, which is not lost by succumbing to the preacher's great temptation to task and prescriptively tell listeners what method will work. Moreover, given the fact that the sermon is occasioned by a special service for children, she does not veer from this central focus. Hope is quantifiably expressed in the preaching act itself. In the end, the audience discovers a preacher, a mother, and a pastor who has found a cause for which she is willing to die.

—CRAFTING STRATEGY: DECOLONIZING THE HOMILETICAL MIND—

In the empire of God (*Baselia tou Theou*) Jesus welcomes persons into personal relationship and fellowship not coercively but by invitation. Yet many preachers remain unthoughtful about how certain interpretations and uses of the New Testament, in the interest of religious expansion, actually prop up imperialism. Fear baits listeners when preachers deploy imperialistic conversion tactics, and consequently kingdom ethics and true discipleship take a backseat. Anti-colonial readings such as Mark 10:15 (*whoever does not accept the empire of God as a little child will not enter it*) of the New Testament function to subvert the status quo, but those unwilling to share or part with wealth face an even more insurmountable challenge.

CST1: HONESTLY EVALUATE YOUR OWN THEOLOGICAL VISION AND HOMILETICAL METHODS OF MISSIONS AND EVANGELISM.

Because persons of color early on are taught to read life racially, that is, to define themselves culturally and racially against unrelenting patterns of comparisons and false perceptions of White privilege birthed in colonialism, it is crucial that preachers of color be especially vigilant in helping hearers see Jesus rightly as one who renders individuals capable of reframing their own visual ecology to see themselves as God's beautiful ones in a socially fragmented age.[24]

CST2: TIE TOGETHER "SOUL WINNING, DISCIPLING FOR CHRIST" COMMITMENTS WITH PRACTICAL TOOLS FOR EQUIPPING CONVERTS TO BE JUSTICE FIGHTERS AGAINST HUMAN EXPLOITATION IN THEIR CONTEXTS.

Global evangelism without prophetic core commitments is gospel deficient and more socially regressive than politically liberative. One way to think about re-orienting one's approach might mean setting up roundtables to discuss what a community's most pressing material needs are and how that particular community perceives its leaders in that context. In their book *The Sermon without End* (Abingdon) homileticians Ron J. Allen and O. Wesley Allen Jr. stir the pot a bit in this regard, calling for apologetics-driven[25] preachers of

---

24. A great essay to read regarding this matter is Willie Jennings's "The Aesthetic Struggle and Ecclesial Vision," *Black Practical Theology* (Waco, TX: Baylor University Press, 2015).

25. In the service of mission and evangelism, Allen and Allen define *apologetics* as a theological/homiletical approach that uses the categories of knowledge, thinking, and values of the contemporary culture to explain and defend Christian faith in response to explicit or implicit

every theological stripe—conservative evangelical, liberal, and post-liberal—to consider collaborating with diverse communities in a *post-apologetic* manner in a social climate of religiously disaffected persons. What they argue is that theological camps not be so wedded to an "all or nothing" apologetic method. A chief aim of apologetics, they note, is to seek either to disapprove the claims of the other or to retreat from authentic dialogue with the wider culture. Allen and Allen rightly claim that to pursue evangelism or missions in either of these ways leaves little room for conversation and learning from different theological perspectives. While collaborative group approaches may not work in every case, especially if one believes that some or most messages are grasped by the preacher's cloistering with God alone as did Moses on Mt. Sinai, soul-winners do well to remain attuned to the heartbeat of the culture.

---

misunderstanding, challenges, and attacks in order to commend that very faith. By contrast, *post-apologetics* . . . brings Christian faith and postmodern pluralism into reciprocal conversation in order that both might be commended to the other and each might critique the other by mutually engaging their categories of and sources for making meaning, practices and experiences, and ethical values. Cf. Ron J. Allen and O. Wesley Allen Jr., *The Sermon without End* (Nashville: Abingdon, 2015), 2, 80.

➜ **EXERCISE** ⬅

Revisit three mission- and evangelism-focused sermons. With each sermon articulate three concrete action steps that congregants can act upon in a practical way (e.g., rotate shifts weekly taking care packages to a battered women's shelter; organize a jobs for guns campaign; package medical kits for a third-world village and with the promise to return to provide academic mentoring, tuition assistance, and scholarships for village citizen(s) to attend nursing or medical school; enlist working professionals in congregation to do pro bono work for a set number of persons as a ministry tithe to the church; write curricula for doing counterintuitive missions in materially privileged European countries and Euro-American communities, many of which consist of large segments of self-professed agnostics and atheists).

In hurting communities, *Exodus preaching is always a word that speaks to the predicament of human suffering and remains interminably hopeful when confronted with communal despair.* Sermons attentive to this mark know that justice is not just about "us." In the next chapter we turn our focus to the importance of preachers connecting homiletic speech to direct action in pursuit of helping others to do likewise.

Chapter Four

NAMING REALITY IN A TONE-DEAF CULTURE

Make sure your nonprofit doesn't make you a non-prophet.

—Raphael G. Warnock

Preachers preach to flesh-and-blood human beings—to humans in communities with particular histories of struggle. Whether helping these faith communities to access and interpret their communal story in light of an ancestral memory of forced migration, such as the transatlantic slave trade, or a group's present-day corporate concern about the disposability of Black lives in poor communities where prospects for human flourishing remain bleak, preachers are tasked to announce God's vision for human flourishing in a world come of age. To name reality is to identify root causes of injustice, concretely pointing out places where society's most vulnerable populations are caught in the crosswinds of greed, violence, and abuses of power.

Exodus preaching connects the speech act with just actions as concrete praxis to help people freely participate in naming their reality.

In many instances, especially in historic churches with legacies of high civic engagement, preachers, unavoidably so, are expected to be social activists, community organizers, and the congregation's lead informant, fulfilling roles often taken for granted in communities characterized as economically robust and culturally privileged. A social activist, for example, is a minister who "insists on the release of various goods and services to be used for community empowerment and giving assistance to those individuals on the margins of society."[1] As one would expect, ministers occupying this socio-functional identity criticize "liturgical practices that do not prepare or prompt individuals to actively engage larger community concerns" such as "racial profiling, homelessness, poverty, gender discrimination, rape, domestic abuse, etc."[2] Social activist preachers such as Traci Blackmon, Frederick D. Haynes III, and William Barber II typically choreograph their messages and employ grassroots organizing skills to generate concern around particular events or issues they believe a congregation should care about.

As one would expect, when the preacher's message is consistent with what it broadcasts the sermon likely secures positive reception and thus achieves greater buy-in to fulfill a certain goal or purposed end. Activist preachers insist that their listeners understand that "Christians have a [far] greater obligation than other persons of good will to develop a social consciousness around the work of alleviating human suffering and rebuilding lives of the marginalized, and challenging systems that endorse oppressive acts."[3]

—CRAFTING STRATEGY: SEEING THE BIGGER PICTURE—

CST1: INTERPRET A SELECTED SCRIPTURAL PASSAGE FOR PREACHING AND KEEP IN MIND HOW DIVINE JUSTICE IS CONCEPTUALLY DEPICTED IN THE TEXT.

Ancient to contemporary hermeneutical transfer is no small matter. When preachers are not theologically critical in their biblical reflection, the God of scripture will be narrowly portrayed as a merciless, politically partisan avenger inflicting punishment on nations who stand in Israel's way or, by contrast, a

---

1.   Kenyatta R. Gilbert, *The Journey and Promise of African American Preaching* (Minneapolis: Fortress, 2011), 134.

2.   Ibid.

3.   Ibid., 137.

benevolent sovereign with indiscriminating compassion without regard for perpetrated offenses against human life and community.

Divine justice may be framed in at least two ways. Therefore, thinking critically about the dual nature of the principle of justice is crucial if preachers are to judiciously appropriate and attach meaning to texts for present-day concerns. On the one hand, for example, in the plague accounts beginning in Exodus 7, in the prohibitions set down in Deuteronomy 28, or in Micah 2:1-3, as sovereign deity who plots and plans treacherous deeds against those who exercise evil, God, the law giver, is depicted as the righteous warrior who metes out justice through the law of retaliation "lex talionis" (deutronomistic theology of retribution). This is a popular view among ancient Near Eastern society and central to the Israelite understanding of justice. Justice, in this sense, equates to retributive and punitive judgment against persons, communities, and nations who practice evil or frustrate God's purposes.[4]

But not all Old Testament passages present the justice of God along punitive lines. In stories such as Cain slaying his brother Abel or Joseph coming to the rescue of his famine-stricken brothers who abandoned him and left him for dead in Genesis, God exercises justice compassionately, and offenses are confronted but restoration to community is still made possible (deuteronomistic theology of love and compassion). Another passage of this sort, Deuteronomy 6:1-9 (compare with Jesus's teaching on the great commandment in the law recorded in Matt 22:34-40), in fact, provides the basis for Jesus's theological orientation toward justice—one of holy rage but even holier compassion. But still the irony here is that Jesus's version of justice is harder for contemporaries to embrace because its theological content is preconditioned by a concern for the transgressor.

Opportunity to relationally connect to the grace and mercy of God is not closed off to the law violator in Jesus's approach to the law. Even in the face of his accusers and crucifiers, in him agony is met with compassion for the community, as the Gospel writer records it. The words "Father, forgive them, for they know not what they do" uttered from the cross are theologically significant for understanding who Jesus is.[5] When handling justice-themed passages, whether located in the Torah readings, the prophetic literature, or Gospel writings, the responsible preacher does so thinking theologically critically about what the text says biblically regarding the nature of God, who has come to us as fulfilled and embodied justice for the purposes of saving.

---

4. See Carol J. Dempsey's discussion in chapter 5 titled "Justice and Liberation Attained through Violence" in her book *Justice: A Biblical Perspective* (St. Louis: Chalice, 2008), 9–10, 42.

5. Ibid., 45–61.

CST2: PAINT THE THEOLOGICALLY ROBUST PICTURE OF JESUS'S LOVE AND HIS COMPASSIONATE ORIENTATION OF JUSTICE IN RELATION TO HOW JUSTICE IS DISTINCTLY CONVEYED AND IMPLEMENTED IN BOTH TESTAMENTS.

To give casual attention to the concept of divine justice and fail to see its theologically layered meaning is to amble down a homiletical dead end. Homiletical dead ends little aid the spiritual growth of the gathered-to-be-sent congregation. When preachers fail to rightly perceive the essence of divine justice, they will either find themselves preaching justice too heavy-handedly absent of hope or too cheaply absent of real consequence.

CST3: SEEK TO UNDERSTAND THE RELEVANT AND FACTUAL DETAILS OF CONTEMPORARY SOCIAL OR POLITICAL HAPPENINGS AS THOROUGHLY AS POSSIBLE WHEN DRAWING SUCH DETAILS INTO THE SERMON.

Preachers must speak a crucial witness when circumstances of death and degradation touch human life. But two things are important to understand here. First, the preacher will never exhaust the meaning or varied ways of looking at a singular situation that may call forth the preacher's address. Thus, to address a topic of concern assumes both a risk and a wager. The preacher never names reality in moments where all i's can be dotted and t's crossed.

Second, the preacher is not the only interpreter in the room of sermon listeners and therefore must not overlook the fact that in our media-rich culture listeners can find the matter-of-facts of any issue by simply consulting any credible print or visual media source on their own. The preacher has a chief duty nonetheless that no one in the context of the preaching event is equipped to do: that is, to take the facts of the human situation and theologically translate those facts in light of divine intentionality—what God intends and expects of God's human creation—and to announce how the good news of the gospel, as God's emancipatory witness, might speak to specific human events and happenings in life-giving, transformative ways at that particular hour.

This is what Exodus preaching does. It names reality and takes a risk. It tells the truth about death in the context of fear and death, and ultimately it declares that evil and despair have an appointed end, and that even though, to use Paul's language, "God has chosen to subject God's creation to futility, not by its own choice, but by the one who subjected it" (see Rom 8:20), God will finally redeem it.

Prophetically conscious preaching names reality in spaces of contestation. One can hear on any given Sunday a preacher inject controversial inserts into their sermons. Clearly, some issues are far more challenging than others to address from the pulpit. On the face of it, one could be biblically faithful to scripture and present logical supports for virtually any perspective on an issue of controversy, but I think it is especially important to be hermeneutically responsible and theologically self-critical when engaging, for example, topics on human sexuality and matters pertaining to sexual orientation.

Before yielding to the temptation of inserting one- or two-line controversial remarks into the sermon, consider the following.

CST4: ADDRESS CONTROVERSIAL TOPICS WITH THE WILL TO ENTER HEALTHY AND RESPECTFUL DISCUSSION ABOUT YOUR PERSPECTIVE WITHOUT DEMONIZING THE OTHERS'.

When naming reality to connect the speech-act with concrete praxis, the question every prophetically conscious preacher has to grapple with is, how does what I preach affirm and protect the hearer's human dignity and personhood? *Exodus preaching is humanizing speech.* Too often preachers, in taking firm stances on religio-political controversial issues, fail to demonstrate how their biblical and theological positions align with Jesus's inaugural vision or concretely point listeners to paths of achieving spiritual wholeness, physical survival, and psychic wellness in tandem with moral concerns and ethical prescriptions. In proclamation, the preacher has to take the hermeneutical risk of not only saying what the text "says," but also take a theologically responsible stab at teaching listeners "how a text means" and why one's perspective on what a text communicates matters.

CST5: FIND THEOLOGICALLY CONSTRUCTIVE WAYS TO DECENTER THE PROGRESSIVE VERSUS CONSERVATIVE BATTLE (IDOLATRY OF PERSPECTIVE).

I teach and worship in spaces of intense theological debate on issues that have divided and splintered churches. So I approach my vocation as teacher-facilitator with a great deal of openness. In short, I mostly moderate these intense debates without imposing on others my theological will or views on certain subjects. I do not say this to hedge because I think that persons often must come to their work not as moderators but as apologists. Preachers fight for theological turf, and in our times, they should. But not all preachers are homiletically responsible.

There's no one way to parse a text, nor is there only one way to see a text. Most hold on to hermeneutical biases and prejudices unless persuaded to do otherwise. We preachers often come to the texts we interpret jaded, closed, too open, or frankly, hermeneutically apathetic. Whatever the case, the preacher's best friend is self-criticism. Idolizing texts and privileging theologies that are provisional at best often lead us down the road of self-serving behaviors and homiletical arrogance.

However, we are still responsible for what we believe in our hearts and confess with our mouths. The most basic task of the preacher is to wrestle with the text listening for what God might be saying to us, through us, for the benefit of others. Again, a sound way of checking oneself self-critically is to see if the message you are called to preach aligns with Jesus's inaugural vision, the Sermon on the Mount, and is grounded in and founded upon God's promise to re-create/renew all things in Christ Jesus, the crucified and risen Savior of the world. In his anointed and humanizing vision, there's empathy, courageous witness, care, assurance, exhortation, hope, vulnerability, sacrifice, obligation, invitation, wisdom, and blessing.

How civically engaged clerics go about their community-building work may differ from one minister to the next. One preacher might believe working alongside the voiceless and nameless members of society requires persistent agitation through highly charged acts of public protests, while another might take the view that such methods do little to turn the political dial and perhaps shut down communication altogether. Clerico-politicians, different from the social activist cleric, tend to undertake their homiletical assignments believing that the people and their communities are best served when preachers work within the system "through legislative processes, lobbying, political antagonism, and creating governmental and fiduciary alliances" with influential political leaders and policy makers.[6] If the preacher wears the social activist mask, the preacher will want to guard against self-deception and tendencies toward self-righteousness; and if the clerico-politician mask is assumed, that preacher must take special care to steer clear of tendencies "to blur the lines of church-state relations, or to allow partisan politics or the quest for greater influence and power to overshadow his or her ministerial charge to be the community's priest."[7]

SERMONIC EXAMPLE
Raphael G. Warnock
"Your Kingdom Come, Your Will be Done"; Matthew 6:10
Ebenezer Baptist Church
Atlanta, GA
2013[8]

---

6.   Ibid., 136.

7.   Ibid., 137.

8.   Original manuscript. See the Supreme Court justices' opinions at http://www.supreme

Ebenezer Baptist Church in Atlanta, Georgia, is probably best known as the home church of its late co-pastor, Reverend Dr. Martin Luther King Jr, as well as his father, Martin Luther King Sr. This association makes Ebenezer a destination spot for countless visitors from around the world. The Kings Sr. and Jr. both built a legacy of social justice preaching and political engagement that continues today under its current pastor, Reverend Dr. Raphael G. Warnock.

Through preaching and teaching rooted firmly in the tradition of liberation theology, Warnock, like his predecessors, without fear directly addresses discriminatory practices and unjust social policies that afflict the lives and suppress the well-being of minority communities, especially its poor and marginalized citizens. Warnock, for example, advocated for the release of Genarlow Wilson and Troy Davis after perceiving their imprisonment as a social injustice. A deeply involved national spokesperson in the "stop the gun violence" movement, Warnock also heads up the Moral Mondays movement in Georgia in affiliation with the NAACP.

In the midst of an economic depression, in 2012, Ebenezer built an $8 million dollar structure to house the Martin Luther King Sr. Community Resource Complex. In addition to providing administrative office space, conference rooms, a new fellowship hall and kitchen, the complex is home to four non-profits that support lower-income families and individuals—Casey Family Programs, Catholic Charities Atlanta, Operation HOPE, and the Center for Working Families Inc. These entities have helped to expand Ebenezer's ministry to members of Ebenezer and the broader community. The Ebenezer pulpit is out front on matters of social protest and local and national politics. Viewing liberation as a central theme of the gospel, Warnock intentionally structures sermons to reach a broad constituency in his preaching, making special appeals to the more sophisticated listeners to actively participate in the public debates.[9]

---

court.gov/opinions/12pdf/12-96_6k47.pdf. Sermon delivered at Ebenezer Baptist Church in Atlanta, Georgia, at the 11 a.m. service on June 30, 2013, the Sunday following the *Shelby County v. Holder, Attorney General, et al,* Supreme Court ruling, which was argued February 27, 2013, and decided on June 25, 2013.

9. "The Preached Word: Holistic Practices in Urban/Suburban Churches" (Metropolitan Atlanta, Ga.) in *Equipping the Saints: Promising Practices in Black Congregational Life's Congregational Resource Guide.* Biographical sketch composed and edited by Kenyatta R. Gilbert and AnneMarie Mingo for *Equipping The Saints,* a Lilly Institute–funded three-year national research project designed to identify, document, and showcase some of the effective practices that contribute to the holistic health and well-being of congregants and communities.

In this sermon that comes from a sermon series on the Lord's Prayer, Warnock weighs in on the Supreme Court's *Shelby County v. Holder* ruling on June 25, 2013, which declared Section 4 of the Voter Rights Act of 1965 unconstitutional. Before calling his congregation to swift action, he centers his topical sermonic reflections on a single verse of scripture. Based on that verse, he makes a declaration followed by a question of its continual validity for Christians in a socially unjust world. He begins,

> What a bold prayer! What a daring prayer! What a revolutionary prayer! Sure, anybody can say it. But can't just anybody pray it and mean it and live it and stand by it. Don't run too swiftly through this prayer. This is a courageous prayer. No, this is a crazy prayer. It takes guts and spiritual nerve to posit this thought and let the universe hear it and respond. How do you pray a prayer like that in a world like this? Thy kingdom come, thy will be done![10]

Like most liberation-focused and -oriented theologians, Warnock reads the passage to confront a matter he believes will have devastating effects on America's poor and politically disenfranchised population. Voicing his frustration with the US legal system, he interprets for his congregation in concrete terms the nature of the *Shelby v. Holder* verdict, and why standing against the establishment's ruling is one's moral and ethical obligation. Distilling out the fine points of the Court's decision, Warnock explains to his economically diverse but mostly formally educated listeners:

> It's hard to see that after last Tuesday. In one fell swoop, five judges stripped away voter protections provided by section 5 of the Voting Rights Act by leaving it in place and striking down section 4. Section 5 provides through the Justice department an important tool called pre-clearance. Any state or area of the country with a history of voter discrimination must pre-clear with the Justice Department any changes it would make in its voting laws. They must be pre-cleared. Section 4 provides the list of nine states, twelve cities, and fifty-seven counties that must pre-clear any changes they would make. Because they struck down Section 4, now nobody is on the list. And the very protections that held at bay SOME of the voter suppression and

---

10. Raphael G. Warnock, "Your Kingdom Come, Your Will Be Done." Unpublished manuscript used by author's permission.

trickery (unnecessary voter ID laws, cutting down early voting, Sunday voting) we saw in 2012 are no longer in place.[11]

Action items for his congregation follow Warnock's assessment of the political battle for justice. Linking prophetic discourse to concrete praxis, he challenges his congregation to take immediate action and see what is at stake when our rights to "equal protection under the law" are threatened. Rev. Warnock declared,

> There are some things *WE CAN DO and MUST DO:* Call your congressperson and senators and demand that they fix section 4 . . . Show up to vote in 2014 . . . Start registering folks to vote now . . . Make use of absentee voting . . . Prepare to sue every state that will institute severe voting restrictions . . . Begin raising money in our churches right now![12]

In the sermon's final move, Warnock declares that Christ's cross is emblematic of the fact that "evil always goes too far!" But in the end, he declares: "Evil will be defeated and the kingdom will surely come."

EVANGELICALISM AND SOCIAL CRITICISM

Preachers wear performative masks they assume to fulfill their ministry obligations. They function as they picture themselves. Who they are and what they do are invariably inseparable. If one self-identifies as an "Evangelical-Moralist,[13] then she or he takes seriously the message of Christianity as recorded in the Bible, holding fast to the hermeneutic that God speaks and is revealed in Scripture."[14] Hence, he or she will likely place strong emphasis on the believer's need to be spiritually converted, baptized, and catechized in demonstration and preparation to have a personal relationship with Jesus Christ. Proselytizing the unchurched and discipling the churched through

---

11. Ibid.

12. These steps are spelled out more specifically on the typed manuscript. See full manuscript in appendix B.

13. This label is a metaphoric construction that seeks to define a minister's social identity and function with a specific religious community. Metaphors can be useful in providing some angle of vision, but at some point they break down when what they describe is taken literally.

14. Gilbert, *Journey and Promise*, 133.

teaching, preaching, and evangelism are nonnegotiable for E-Ms, for this is what it means to honor the Great Commission—to spread the gospel message as a believer throughout the world.

The label *evangelical* can mean a host of things religiously and politically. The term itself has become politically corrupted and has ballooned into a great source of consternation within and without the body of Christ. Its long-standing usage, derived from Greek word *euangelion*, means "good news" or "gospel," and traces from Mark 1:1. However, as a term used in reference to a specific theology movement birthed in the European Reformation that arose in the late nineteenth- and twentiety-century, "evangelical" fundamentalists huddled in reaction against liberal theology's claim that the Bible contains historically inaccurate elements that were disobliging to the modern mind and hence needed to be historically provable to be deemed reliable. Fundamentalists argued that biblical writers, under the auspices of divine inspiration, accurately transmitted the Bible in terms of testimony and events. Defenders of evangelical fundamentalism offered three biblical takeaways for the saints: 1) God inspired the Bible; 2) its contents are internally self-consistent (i.e., God can only be consistent to the degree that the biblical materials agree with one another); and 3) the Bible as "Word of God" is universally true, valid from epoch to epoch, and always applicable. A distinctive five-fold set of fundamentals would define the late twentieth century movement when its defenders broke huddle. Evangelical preachers and teachers held to:

- The inerrancy of the Bible

- The divinity of Jesus

- Substitutionary atonement as the essential work of Christ

- The physical resurrection of Christ

- The literal, physical return of Christ

While holding to a high view of biblical authority and Christian orthodoxy go hand in hand with adherents to evangelical Christianity, not all agree how they understand God to have inspired the Bible's authority. Some maintain the position of total inerrancy—that God essentially dictated the Bible word-for-word without error. Others think that humans have had some role in shaping the Bible's composition. The foremost concern of evangelicals is "bringing people into the ark of salvation" or "safety" if you grew up in my church of birth. And tied to this theological agenda is the sermonic agenda of clarifying what the Bible says and how it applies today.[15]

THORNS AND THISTLES: RELIGIOUS HYPOCRISY AND TRADITION ACCOUNTABILITY

I affirm many of the commitments central to evangelical theology, but I will not shy away from critical commentary. Holding a tradition accountable to a constructive vision for community wellness and restoration in the here-and-now that affirms the personhood and preserves the dignity of all people is very important to me and how I understand and articulate religious faith and share my normative vision of how Christians should live working in partnership with God. It is also important to know that though carrying the same spirit, after World War II and the 1940s, unlike early evangelical fundamentalists who withdrew from public life awaiting Christ's return (God's retribution time to condemn the larger culture outside the household of faith), America's White Evangelical caste became more socially engaged—forming religiously sectarian schools, endorsing and lobbying certain politicians in voting blocs to influence legislation, frequently under the pretense of divine sanction. The battle lines in the sand are as conspicuous as ever along with a flurry of theological contradictions and religious hypocrisy.

How you see your Bible will dictate your politics. Right belief without morally right actions to follow equals retarded faith.

But just as the post-WWII offspring of White fundamentalists were influenced by postwar events of cultural change and academic success, which permitted evangelicals an opportunity to re-invent themselves, so must Black evangelicals re-invent themselves in light of the cultural shifting taking place today—shifting that has dealt disastrous blows to some communities more than others.

Sermons preached by evangelicals of the apologist (defender of the faith) sort tend to be resourced with multiple scriptural citations, draw on major biblical themes, and are clear-cut and prescriptive.

---

15. Ibid., 44-47, 89. Cf. Ronald J. Allen's *Thinking Theologically* (Minneapolis: Fortress, 2008) for a comparative mapping of different theological families.

GENDER BIAS AND PULPIT DISCRIMINATION

One of the great challenges as a preaching professor is helping learners to stretch their theology: namely, how they perceive who God is and convey what God is like in their sermons. This becomes particularly important for African American preachers, especially African American women preachers, because most come from church contexts that overuse exclusively masculine language for God and humanity.

African American women make up more than 70 percent of the active membership of generally any African American congregation one might attend today. According to one Pew study, African American women are among the most religiously committed of the Protestant demographic—eight in 10 say that religion is important to them. Yet, America's Christian pulpits, especially African American pulpits, remain male-dominated spaces. Still today, eyebrows raise, churches split, pews empty, and recommendation letters get lost at a woman's mention that God has called her to preach. The deciding factor for women desiring to pastor and be accorded respect equal to their male counterparts generally whittles down to one question: Can she preach?

The fact is that African American women have preached, formed congregations, and confronted many racial injustices since the slavery era. The earliest Black female preacher was a Methodist woman simply known as Elizabeth. She held her first prayer meeting in Baltimore in 1808 and preached for about fifty years before retiring to Philadelphia to live among the Quakers. An unbroken legacy of African American women preachers persisted even long after Elizabeth. Reverend Jarena Lee became the first African American woman to preach at the African Methodist Episcopal (AME) Church. She had started even before the church was officially formed in the city of Philadelphia in 1816. But, she faced considerable opposition. AME Bishop Richard Allen, who founded the denomination, initially refused Lee's request to preach. It was only upon hearing her speak, presumably, from the floor, during a worship service, that he permitted her to give a sermon. Lee reported that Bishop Allen,

> rose up in the assembly, and related that [she] had called upon him eight years before, asking to be permitted to preach, and that he had put [her] off; but that he now as much believed that [she] was called to that work, as any of the preachers present.

78

Jarena Lee spoke truth to power and paved the way for other mid-to-late nineteenth-century Black female preachers to achieve validation as pulpit leaders, although she never received official clerical appointments. The first woman to achieve this validation was Julia A. J. Foote. In 1884, she became the first woman ordained a deacon in the African Methodist Episcopal Zion AMEZ Church. Shortly after followed the ordinations of AME evangelist Harriet A. Baker, who in 1889 was perhaps the first Black woman to receive a pastoral appointment. Mary J. Small became the first woman to achieve "elder ordination" status, which permitted her to preach, teach, and administer the sacraments of Holy Communion.

Historian Bettye-Collier Thomas maintains that the goal for most Black women seeking ordination in the late nineteenth and early twentieth centuries was simply a matter of gender inclusion, not necessarily pursuing the need to transform the patriarchal church. Today, several respected African American women preachers and teachers of preachers proudly stand on Lee's, Foote's, Baker's, and Small's shoulders raising their prophetic voice.[16] Elizabeth Peter, a seminarian at United Lutheran Seminary, in Harrisburg, Pennsylvania, is one such voice. She is studying to be an ordained pastor in the Evangelical Lutheran Church in America, a denomination where in 2017 nearly 27 percent of clergy on the ELCA roster are women, and 86 out of 456 serve as senior pastors in the ELCA, as she notes in her sermon.

This biblically based law/gospel oriented evangelical message is furnished with clear fact-based statistical data, historical biography, cogent exegetical analysis, and social justice critique.

Things to note:

1. Use of repetition.

2. Data collection.

3. Use of research statistics.

4. Insertion of historical biography.

5. Address to the church.

6. Concrete and contextual application.

---

16.   Kenyatta R. Gilbert, "Hidden Figures: How Black Women Preachers Spoke Truth to Power," *The Conversation*, February 24, 2017, http://theconversation.com/hidden-figures-how-black-women-preachers-spoke-truth-to-power-73185.

7. Hermeneutical shift and organization flow from law to grace (gospel).

8. The striking question, "Who has a seat?" as an organizing principle.

SERMONIC EXAMPLE ➡

Elizabeth Peter
"A Seat at the Table"; Deuteronomy 10:14-17
Howard University School of Divinity
Washington, DC
October 12, 2017[17]

> [14] To the Lord your God belong the heavens, even the highest heavens, the earth and everything in it. [15] Yet the Lord set his affection on your ancestors and loved them, and he chose you, their descendants, above all the nations—as it is today. [16] Circumcise your hearts, therefore, and do not be stiff-necked any longer. [17] For the Lord your God is God of gods and Lord of lords, the great God, mighty and awesome, who shows no partiality and accepts no bribes.

In the night in which He was betrayed our Lord Jesus took the bread, broke it and said this is my body given for you . . . and He looked at all of them seated at the table. He looked to his left and seated next to him was the one who would betray Him, and then to his right—the one who would deny him, and then to the rest of the table—all the ones who would abandon Him, forsake Him. Which disciples come to mind?

Peter, Judas, James, John . . . but what about Mary, Martha?

See, even you don't think of the women. I certainly did not. Jesus did, God did. Jesus, the messiah, the Son of God, revealed His resurrected self to the women first. Women, who weren't allowed to learn

---

17. Original manuscript. This sermon was delivered in my fall 2017 African American Prophetic Preaching course in which Elizabeth Peter enrolled as a visiting consortium student.

how to read or write, weren't allowed to talk to a teacher, who weren't allowed to testify in court were treated like Gentiles, the undesirables, and denied many social privileges. They had all of this going against them, yet God chose them as the first evangelicals. They were first to spread the good news of Jesus' resurrection, and yet this title is stripped from them. Our culture, throughout the years, has removed seats at the tables were women deserve to sit.

God chose them as the first evangelicals. The first to spread the good news of Jesus' resurrection, a new frontier of God's saving grace, and yet . . .

In a new frontier of space exploration in 1962 John Glenn was the first American to orbit the Earth. Proclaimed a national hero for winning the race in getting a human into space. But successfully bringing him back to Earth was no minor feat. There were countless unknown variables in play that made this possible: weightlessness, a new capsule, and of course, the galaxy itself. "Americans collectively *held* their breath as the world's newest pioneer swept across the threshold of one of man's last frontiers."[18] A man's frontier. But what about the women?

I didn't hear about some of the women who played a crucial part in Glenn's successful travel until the book *Hidden Figures* written by Margot Shetterly was published in 2016. Here arrived a book, which finally shined light on African American women who were overlooked during this momentous time in American history.[19] Working for NASA in Langley, Virginia, women worked as human computers, running numbers for engineering calculations while having to battle racism and sexism everyday in the workplace, all to aid in "man's last frontier." These women were integral parts in putting a man into space and fifty-four years later we hear about it.

Katherine Johnson, Dorothy Vaughan, Mary Jackson were not given a seat at the table.

It took sixty-two years for Henrietta Lacks—the woman whose cancer cells have been used to cure polio, to clone, to fight cancer, to

---

18.   Bryan Ethier, "John Glenn: First American to Orbit the Earth," *HistoryNet*, June, 12, 2006, http://www.historynet.com/john-glenn-first-american-to-orbit-the-earth.htm.

19.   Maya Wei-Haas, "The True Story of 'Hidden Figures,' the Forgotten Women Who Helped Win the Space Race," *Smithsonian*, September 8, 2016, http://www.smithsonian mag.com/history/forgotten-black-women-mathematicians-who-helped-win-wars-and-send -astronauts-space-180960393/.

develop vaccines, and to gene map—to finally be recognized for her invaluable contribution to biomedical research. While being treated at John Hopkins, a sample of her cells was taken from her cervix without her consent. And the doctor found her cells, known as HeLa cells, to be remarkable because they wouldn't die.[20] Her cells have been used to study disease and test human sensitivity to new products and substances. We have all benefitted from her cells. She never gave consent. In fact, her family wasn't told until 20 years after the 1951 procedure. Only now have people even been able to put a name to the cells and have begun to acknowledge this woman's momentous contribution to all of our lives.

Henrietta Lacks was not given a seat at the table.

Baptist minister Martin Luther King, Jr., who was the most visible leader in the Civil Rights movement, known for his prophetic speeches, and nonviolent civil disobedience knew firsthand the sufferings of Blacks in this country. As an African American he lived through experiences of dehumanization and the depersonalizing effects of racism.[21] He had a doctrine of dignity that focused on the dignity of his people. But this philosophy broke down when applied to women. In the Southern Christian Leadership Conference, an organization that King headed, there were significant contributions made by Black women that didn't receive acknowledgement. More than Black men, it was Black women who initiated the bus boycott from Montgomery to Memphis. And yet, women were absent from planning sessions held by Black male leadership. They were neither publicly acknowledged by King nor the SCLC leadership for their contributions. Lynn Olson, wrote that "the woman who had shown them the way was denied a voice of her own." Rosa Parks was not invited to ride the desegregated buses. "King and Abernathy, on the day after the Supreme Court ruled against Montgomery's segregation ordinance" failed to include Rosa. "This powerfully symbolic gesture spoke volumes about their attitudes toward key women in the boycott."[22]

Rosa Parks, Ella Baker, Jo Ann Robinson, were all not given a seat at the table.

---

20. "Henrietta Lacks," *Biography*, accessed October 12, 2017, https://www.biography .com/people/henrietta-lacks-21366671.

21. Rufus Burrow Jr., *God and Human Dignity: The Personalism, Theology, and Ethics of Martin Luther King, Jr.* (Notre Dame, IN: University of Notre Dame Press, 2006), 128, 129.

22. Ibid., 131

Throughout our collective history women have continuously gone unacknowledged and uninvited to have a place at the table.

In our scripture today, the word of God reads: *For the Lord your God is God of gods and Lord of lords, he great God, mighty and awesome, who shows no partiality and accepts no bribes.* [18] *He defends the cause of the fatherless and the widow, and loves the foreigner residing among you, giving them food and clothing.* [19] *And you are to love those who are foreigners, for you yourselves were foreigners in Egypt.*

See what's happening here is Moses is encouraging the people of Israel to obey God's law, to obey the Ten Commandments. Because the law gives our lives order and orients us to God. The law tells us over and over again that we need God. The law gives us examples of how to live our lives, and to know that we need God. The law pushes us to the gospel, which shows us that we don't make a place for ourselves at the table, God does.

> But there are laws and orders in this world that
> are not of God—

There is this worldwide phenomenon of a sexual caste—a "planetary sexual caste system [which] involves birth-ascribed hierarchically ordered groups whose members have unequal access to goods, services, and prestige and to physical and mental well-being." Our society has functioned along this "exploitative sexual caste system that could not be perpetuated without the consent of victims as well as the dominant sex, and such consent is obtained through sex role socialization—a conditioning process which begins to operate from the moment we are born, and which is enforced by most institutions." The media, our parents and friends, teachers, books, artists, musicians, clothing manufacturers, psychologists, doctors, Twitter, Instagram, all of this influences us unconsciously and "reinforces the assumptions, attitudes, stereotypes, customs, and arrangements of sexually hierarchical society." Sexual caste is masked by sex role segregation— a complete delusion that women should be "equal but different." [23]

Equal but different doesn't seem to even be true. Women of color make up only 11.9% of managerial and professional positions in the country, Latina women only 3.9% of that and African-American women

---

23.   Mary Daly, *Beyond God the Father: Toward a Philosophy of Women's Liberation,* rev. ed. (Boston: Beacon Press, 1993), 3.

5.3%.[24] You may be thinking that "well that's just the corporate world, the church isn't like that." I was thinking exactly the same thing until I saw that pastoral leadership doesn't get any better. "In 2017, nearly 27% of clergy on the ELCA roster were women. When it comes to senior leadership 9 out of 65 synod bishops are women while 86 out of 456 are senior pastors in the ELCA. The 2015 survey found that 23.3 percent of men whose recent call is their fourth or subsequent are paid above synod guidelines, compared to 13.7 percent of women."[25]

By not being seated at the table, by not having a voice where it is dominated by men, women have been "deprived of power, potency, creativity, and ability to communicate."[26] The ability to share the good news of the resurrected one! And so we must ask ourselves—who has a seat at the table? And in this world, we have many tables. Tables in our classrooms, tables in our boardrooms, tables in our homes and houses—and yes even in the white ones . . .

In Jesus's time powerful ministry took place around tables—particularly around those with a meal. In the ancient world people saw the sharing of meals as having eternal consequences. If you ate meals with the right kind of people paradise awaited you. If you ate with the wrong kind of people...well, something far from paradise. But we often find Jesus breaking bread with the have-nots—the "sinners" and outcasts of his world. Jesus was radical. He challenges the culture and tells us to invite the "poor, the crippled, the lame, the blind to our meals" (Lk 14:13). Today when we think about who is invited to our table do we even think about those who are the outcasts? Do we think about the *fatherless and the orphaned, the widowed and the foreigner?* We just may be those people who want a seat at the table too. Sitting at the table with Christ means we have to share our most intimate moments with society's outer rim. It means we have to let prejudices and negative judgments die, let go of social hierarchy, economic gaps, gender biases, and be present at the table alongside Jesus Christ.

It is in vain if we worship right next to someone and remain silent to the hatred going on around us. It is in vain if we worship and

---

24. "We Have a Women's Leadership Problem—and It's Not for the Reasons You Think," *Everyday Feminism,* October 19, 2015, https://everydayfeminism.com/2015/10/womens -leadership-problem/.

25. Erin Strybis, "Women Clergy Thankful for Gains, Frustrated by Leadership Gap," *Living Lutheran,* February 23, 2016, https://www.livinglutheran.org/2016/02/women-clergy -thankful-for-gains-frustrated-leadership-gap/.

26. Daly, *Beyond God the Father,* 9.

continue to teach misogyny and bigotry to our children. It is in vain if we stay *silent* and not raise up female leaders to help change our world. We have chosen to be partial. We have chosen to stay silent.

As sinners God still gives us a seat at the table. And do we deserve it? No! The law convicts us, the law shows us how easily we fail to keep God's commandments. Rather, it is because of the Gospel, the life, death, and resurrection of Jesus Christ, the love and grace that God has shown us. The fact that God is not partial to us is a serious relief! If it were left to humans to decide who would have a seat at the table very few of us would be there.

The Lord has set the table. The Lord has poured us the cup of salvation filled with Christ's blood, filled with an everlasting covenant, forgiveness, grace, and love. And the table is set, with a seat for you and me.

—CRAFTING STRATEGY: MAPPING THE MESSAGE—

Getting at the facts and noting what information is available on a public issue is a crucial step in this initial stage as well. While many in the congregation may have a certain expertise on a public issue, scanning newspapers, combing the Internet, watching television, and reviewing academic journals aids the preacher's preparation and deepens the preacher's wisdom as well. Finally, engage the scriptures, first reading and prayerfully meditating on the text devotionally. Take note of surfacing details and images that present early on, and then paraphrase the text in your own words.

CST 1: WRITE A TOPIC PROPOSAL BUILDING FROM YOUR INFORMATION GATHERING.

SUGGESTED WRITING OUTLINE

The topic I will be reflecting on is . . .

It is an important topic for the following reasons:

Some of the details and statistical facts about this (public issue or ecclesial concern) are as follows:

1.

2.

3.

I think the church and religious leaders are silent on this issue because . . .

A better understanding and thoughtful engagement of this issue might bring about . . .

||||||||||||||||||||||||||||||||||||||||||||||||||||||||||||||||||||||||||||||||||||||||||||||||||||||||||||||||||||||||||||||||||||||||||||||||||||||

Given our culture's propensity to silence victims of circumstance and trivialize their suffering plight, *Exodus preaching connects concrete speech with just actions as concrete praxis to help people freely participate in naming their reality.* Prophetic discourse dares to speak about God's presence in spaces where pain, oppression, and despair are all too apparent. Sermons and strategies in the next chapter attend to the preacher's certain disposition toward the power and beauty of Black oral expression.

EXERCISE

Statistical data sheet openings disrupt convention (data can be reported in a negative or positive light). Seek to disrupt conventional approaches. This can be a good thing if thoughtfully done. Simply detailing alarming and distressing concerns first and stating the hypothetical positives or literal positives is too predictable and communicates that the sermon majors in problems to solve.

Research *three* controversial or distressing issues. After data collection write down a fact issue statement painting a less than ideal scenario, as a media pundit would report on an issue. Now ask yourself, "Can I flip listener perception with unanticipated statements that can reframe an issue to be heard in a different way?"

For example:

Predictable statement:

One of every three Black males born today can expect to go to prison in his lifetime.[27]

Unpredictable statements:

One out of three Black boys will go to college.

Three out of four Black men don't do drugs.

Seven out of eight aren't teenage fathers.

Eleven out of twelve won't drop out of high school.

Five out of nine have a job.[28]

---

27. Quoted in Tavis Smiley's *Covenant with Black America* (Chicago: Third World, 2006), 53.

28. "I Am a Statistic," NAACP documentary, January 26, 2015, YouTube video, 0:31, posted by McGoldrick Marketing, https://youtu.be/HgVNsCLd8iY.

INVENTIVE SPEECH AND POETIC PERCEPTIONS

Preaching is communication in the concrete, filled with language and images from day-to-day details—dynamics, sights, sounds, smells, tastes, texture, and life scenes.

—Teresa L. Fry Brown[1]

Whether a person of color or not, if asked the question, "How would you describe African American preaching?" many would describe this genre of preaching as theatrical, performance-driven, energetic, bombastic, showy, soul-stirring, ornamental, and Jesus-centered. And if persons were to visit any number of Black congregations in the United States today as first-timers, their description would not be far afield and perhaps a fair deduction. However, it is more than accurate to say that such descriptors are woefully deficient when attempting to obtain an appropriate picture of the nature and function of Black preaching. What is often missed is the broad range of techniques, approaches, modes, and styles of preaching that sit under the canopy of the Black preaching tradition that contrast with Eurocentric preaching traditions or preaching practices developed by non-European people groups. Because the wider culture and younger generations of African Americans remain badly informed about what Black preaching is, I have arrived at at least a working definition. So before proceeding, it is important that a fuller picture of the tradition is

---

1. Teresa L. Fry Brown, *Delivering the Sermon* (Minneapolis: Fortress, 2008), 8.

presented to address deficiencies in understanding. Otherwise, first-timers will have a malformed picture of what Black preaching truly is.

When I use the term *African American preaching*, I am referring to *a ministry of Christian proclamation—a theorhetorical discourse about God's goodwill toward community with regard to divine intentionality, communal care, and the active practice of hope—that finds resources internal to Black life in the North American context.*[2] The aspect of the discourse specifically emphasized in this book is the prophetic dimension—the dimension rooted in the principles of justice and hope that convey an outlook of divine purpose. One distinctive hallmark of African American prophetic preaching is its poetic character; it not only speaks concretely to situations of tragedy and despair, but it does so in daringly evocative and creative ways, drawing on the beauty of language and culture.

||||||||||||||||||||||||||||||||||||||||||||||||||||||||||||||||||||||||||||||||||||||||||||||||||||||||||||||||||||||||||||||||||

Exodus preaching carries an impulse for beauty in its use of language and culture.

||||||||||||||||||||||||||||||||||||||||||||||||||||||||||||||||||||||||||||||||||||||||||||||||||||||||||||||||||||||||||||||||||

—CRAFTING STRATEGY: USING POETRY AND LITERATURE AS SERMON PRE-TEXT OR ACCENT—

The preacher's task as the prophetic messenger of God is to cast figurative symbols that appeal to the imagination. The preacher must value words and relish the beauty of how words speak worlds into existence. The African American prophet has had a particular disposition toward using adorned speech to connect with listeners in ways that flattened prose cannot. Sermonic prose principally carries out an informational function with propositional speech as its tool and intellectual enlightenment as its primary goal.

Martin L. King Jr.'s quotes have been used to good effect in contemporary preaching. But with King's more popular quotes such as "We are caught in an inescapability network of mutuality, tied in a single garment of destiny. Whatever affects one directly, affects all indirectly" enlivening a great many sermons heard succeeding his death, the prophetically conscious preacher must take care to avoid flatlining a sermon by overusing or thoughtlessly dumping exquisitely crafted quotes incautiously into a sermon. Below are seldom-used captivating quotes penned or spoken by Dr. King.

---

2. Kenyatta R. Gilbert, *The Journey and Promise of African American Preaching* (Minneapolis: Fortress, 2011), 11.

"Without love, benevolence becomes egotism and martyrdom becomes spiritual pride."

"Death is not the ultimate evil: the ultimate evil is to be outside God's love."
—*Strength to Love*

"Out of a mountain of despair, a stone of hope."
—"I Have a Dream" Speech

King quoting others in "A Knock at Midnight":

"No lie can live forever."—Carlyle

"Truth, crushed to earth, will rise again."—William Cullen Bryant

"Truth forever on the scaffold,

Wrong forever on the throne.

Yet that scaffold sways the future.

Behind the dim unknown stands God,

Within the shadow keeping watch above his own."—James Russell Lowell

"Let judgment roll down as waters, and righteousness as a mighty stream."
—Amos

"Love your enemies."—Jesus

SERMONIC EXAMPLE →

Jennifer Watley Maxell
"A Dream Deferred: A Theology of Hope"[3]
Canon Chapel, Emory University
Atlanta, GA

---

3.   Original manuscript. Sermon was delivered at Emory University's Canon Chapel on April 18, 2013.

Reverend Jennifer Watley Maxell is a minister, educator, and co-founder of the Breakthrough Fellowship in Cobb County, Georgia—a church initiative that she and her husband, Charles A. Maxell Jr., founded with the blessings of Bishop William P. DeVeux, presiding prelate of the Sixth Episcopal District of the AME Church. Although Maxell is a newly licensed preacher and freshly minted seminary graduate, she is "a child of the manse"—the daughter of the Reverend Dr. William D. Watley, the senior pastor of St. Phillip AME Church in Atlanta, Georgia, and Mrs. Muriel Lewis Watley. Dr. William Watley, an esteemed veteran preacher, formerly pastored the St. James AME Church in Newark, New Jersey, and co-authored *Sermons from the Black Pulpit* with Dr. Samuel D. Proctor. Jennifer Maxell is also the elder sibling of the Rev. Matthew L. Watley, executive minister of Reid Temple AME Church (North Campus) in Silver Spring, Maryland. In a sermon she preached before her professors and seminary peers at Candler Seminary in Atlanta, Watley intones Langston Hughes's probing, yet sobering question, "What happens to a dream deferred?"

A DREAM DEFERRED: A THEOLOGY OF HOPE

HARLEM

BY LANGSTON HUGHES

> What happens to a dream deferred?
>   Does it dry up
>   like a raisin in the sun?

In this iconic poem written by Langston Hughes, the poet is inviting the reader to ponder the destiny of an unactualized dream. However, more than musing about the plight of an individual whose dream is deferred, the poet is engaging the question of community and the fate of a community when its dreams are deferred. While individual dreams being deferred are bad enough, the myriad calamities that ensue when an entire community is stripped of its dreams and left with life as we know it are cataclysmic at best.

Whether the community dries up "like a raisin in the sun" like Detroit, whose blocks of abandoned homes and businesses speak of the booming automotive industry of times past; or

Whether it "festers like a sore and then runs" like Harlem, whose gleaming, gentrified areas are unable to stave off the bloodletting in its most depressed areas; or

Whether it "stinks like rotten meat" like the Pittsburgh neighborhood of Atlanta, where sex trafficking, drugs, and violent crime run rampant in the shadows of the lights and the family fun of Turner Field; or

Whether it "crusts and sugars over" like New York City, where police brutality still adversely affects the Blacks and the Browns despite their international claims of multiethnic diversity; or

Whether it "sags like a heavy load" like the US economy, that still operates at a suppressed rate for the lower and middle class while the upper class makes billions and gets rewarded with a lower tax rate; or

It explodes like the pristine, tree-lined streets of Newtown, Connecticut . . .

Our experience tells us that a dream deferred is simply no good.

The writer of Proverbs 29:18a in the KJV puts it this way, "Where there is no vision, the people perish." The question must then be asked why are our communities drying up, festering, stinking, and exploding when we seem to be surrounded by visionaries. In a society filled with visionaries such as media mogul Oprah Winfrey, new-school captains of industry like Mark Zuckerberg, international leaders like President Barack Obama, committed politicians like Mayor Kaseem Reid, community activists, parents, preachers, professors, and yes even seminarians, why are our cities, our communities, struggling to survive? During a time of technological innovation and economic growth for some, why do so many still find themselves on the outside peering through the window of the American dream?

I submit to you that the answer is a complicated one that requires more than a cursory rehashing of our societal problems and ills. It is an answer that challenges us to confront our polarized political positions and agendas and forces us to "read, reread, and read again" what thus says the Lord in order to find what we may have missed the first two times. Lack of vision, which I'm categorizing as "dreams deferred," is one of the main reasons why our communities are suffering and the church's unwillingness to think outside the box and reimagine new possibilities is one of the reasons why we, that's me and you, aren't helping.

Our over-reliance on tradition, orthodoxy, and theory are stifling our ability to be theologically innovative and responsive in practice. In this morning's text a prophet named Samuel recorded a short period in the history of Israel and wrote about a king named Saul and his son Jonathan. Saul and Jonathan are unique characters in the history of Israel in that they were the first king and heir to the throne respectively. Though one would expect that Jonathan would inherit his father's throne, that privilege was essentially taken from him and given to the son of a shepherd named David when Saul's kingship was undermined, by his own hand.

Samuel gives us a glimpse of these two individuals and their unique relationship. The Israelites were at war with the Philistines who were warrior giants that inhabited the land that God had promised Israel. It was God's desire to establish Israel as a nation that would reflect God's character; and through them bring all the nations to God's own self. On the other hand, the Philistines were convinced that their gods were more powerful than the God of Israel, and so a war raged between the two kingdoms.

As warrior-king, Saul had the vision and the responsibility to lead the charge. If you read through 1 Samuel 7, you will discover that Saul had been commanded by the Lord God God's self to engage in battle and was promised a sure victory; yet in the text we find Saul under the pomegranate tree not engaged in battle. With Israel's army, the priest, and the Ark of the Covenant at his side Saul still seems to sit idly by not engaging in battle. Saul's position reminds me of some of us who consider ourselves to be the progenitors of tradition and hoard church, denominational and, yes, even academic capital, authority, and influence rather than use it to save our communities. A dream deferred or shall I say a dream hoarded. Despite the fact that God had given him the vision of a victorious Israel, Saul remained complacent under a pomegranate tree while his son Jonathan and his armor bearer stole away to the Philistine garrison.

Jonathan for his part often fares better in the retelling and teaching of this story. His decision to take his armor bearer and confront the Philistine army legitimately speaks of his great faith and courage, allowing him to be the hero. His rebelliousness at sneaking away and lack of a real battle plan are often overshadowed by Israel's eventual defeat of the Philistines. While often amounting to bad practice and bad theology, in this case the end truly does seem to justify the means. Like those of us "Starbucks" Christians, too cool for robes, orthodoxy and pipe organs, focused on making the church accessible to the world, we sometimes become so enamored with our own theological rhetoric and acoustic or hip-hop melodies that we become ineffective at real change because we have no foundation and no plan. A dream deferred, or in this case, just a dream with no actualization.

While the traditional dichotomy of Saul's procrastination and Jonathan's perseverance, Saul's complacency and Jonathan's initiative, Saul's fear and Jonathan's courage, Saul's immobility and Jonathan's action, Saul's apathy and Jonathan's conviction, and Saul's doubt and Jonathan's faith has merit. I submit that this polarizing view is not the only one. While Saul serves as the proverbial "don't" in terms of faith in action and Jonathan seems to serve as the proverbial "do," the lessons gleaned from their story don't end there. By backing up and rereading the text we can see another perspective of this relationship come into view. Instead of seeing Saul and Jonathan as people whose response to this situation put them at odds with each other, we can see two people, occupying different places in the story whose participation are both integral to the conclusion.

By that I mean that Saul's vision and promise of victory led him to position Israel's troops in close proximity of the Philistine garrison. Although he failed to lead the charge into battle, Jonathan takes up that task and along with his armor bearer strikes the offensive blow that sends the Philistines running. God then initiates a panic which alerts Saul who charges in with the army and Hebrew neighbors to secure the victory that day. Rather than a two-dimensional enactment of Jonathan's victory, this reinterpretation gives us a panoramic view wherein God uses Jonathan, his armor bearer, Saul, the Israelite army, and neighboring Hebrews to secure the victory.

The conventional interpretation of this narrative, which pits Saul the procrastinator against Jonathan the conqueror serves as a kind of morality tale that teaches us valuable lessons about our individual responses of action or inaction. Clearly juxtaposed against Saul, Jonathan's faithful and courageous confrontation of the Philistines is the way to go. We learn that that our responsibility as theologians and practitioners of faith requires more than distanced commentary and contemplation in response to God's vision for our lives. We are all called to be active participants fully engaged in God's work in the world. We each have a responsibility to leave the cloistered world of the "pomegranate tree," to get into our communities and secure the victory as promised by God.

However, we should also hold in tension our expectation of Jonathan. While heroic and faithful, he isn't necessarily the "savior of the day." By ascribing this characteristic to him we become shortsighted to all of the other factors and players that bring this victory to fruition and reinforce the idea that we as individuals have the power in our own hands to save our communities. While like Jonathan, we are called to be courageous people of faith, audacious enough to stand on God's word and do something spectacular, we must also guard against a sense of rugged individualism that maintains that the solutions to our community problems lay in our capabilities as individuals.

You see, my goal isn't to throw away the conventional interpretation of this story but rather to reinterpret or reimagine or re-dream it if you will. To interpret it in a way that is both innovative and practical. The true mark of innovation isn't the creation of something new. The true mark of innovation is to make changes to something already established using new methods, ideas, theologies, interpretations, or practices. Innovation requires a community of unique and dissimilar individuals coming together with the same goal in mind. The polarizing effects of our inability to recognize each other's intrinsic value and giftedness as children of God is stifling our ability to be innovative and deferring the dreams of our communities both large and small. While large cities with their large-scale problems are some of the easiest to recognize, by rereading our own context we are able to incline our eye to see our own problems afresh.

When we look at our own community where certain people only attend chapel on certain days, where people who sit in classes together for years don't even speak to each other in passing, where food is eagerly given away to shelters and the homeless yet students with strained budgets can't even get a cheap cup of coffee, we must ask ourselves about our own dreams deferred. In what ways is our clinging to the tradition of who we were or who we wanted to be impeding our ability to be the best of who we are?

While this word may seem sobering and hopeless, I suggest that it is anything but. You see, Langston Hughes's poem is titled "A Dream Deferred" and not "A Dream Dead," which lets me know that all hope is not lost. More than simply questioning what happens in communities when dreams are put off or deferred, the poet is imploring us to dream, to reimagine, to reinterpret, to innovate. Just because the dream is deferred, doesn't mean that it's dead and since it's not dead there is hope. And that's the good news I bring to you here in this community called Candler this day. Just because the dream has been deferred, doesn't mean that it's dead.

When Saul sat idly under the pomegranate tree, the story could've been over, but God raised up Jonathan. When Jonathan and his armor bearer beat the twenty Philistines, the story could've been over, but God sent a panic and the Philistines went running, which could've ended the story, but then God moved Saul and the army into position to swoop down on the Philistines. When they moved, God sent in the neighboring Hebrews to help secure the victory. The community dream of victory over the Philistines was won by God's use of the community. And that's good news because it tells us that we all have a stake, a share, a claim, a contribution in the flourishing of our communities.

Whether you procrastinated your way through HT and find your grade lower than you'd like, I'm here to let you know that the semester isn't over. There's still time to get yourself in gear and raise that grade. Whether you've neglected the articles that you promised yourself you'd submit, the semester's not over, there's still time to get it in. Whether you've missed the opportunity to take certain classes or professors before you graduate, there's still time to audit as an alumnus. Whether you refused to accept that bill from the ever-persistent creditor, there's still time to renegotiate your terms. Whether it took you well into your mid-life years to receive and accept your call, there's still time to live out your vocation in a way that is pleasing to God.

Regardless of your situation, I know that there's still time because God always has a Saul encamped over yonder with an army who will help you fight the battle, or a Jonathan who will steal off and strike a blow on your behalf or some Hebrew neighbors who will have your back when it really matters. When we feel hopeless and are sitting under our "pomegranate trees" of regret, despair, and dreams deferred, God sends us a community to help hold our hope.

Now I know some of you say that's all well and good but my situation is too far gone for the community's help. Let me tell you that I hear you and I feel you. I've been there too myself when no amount of hand-holding, hookups, hugs, or innovation from the community would do, when all I could do was fall on my knees and cry out. That's when God Godself stepped through time and space, came wrapped in human flesh, suffered, bled, and died for my sins. Now let's be clear: while that is all well and good, the best part is that on the third day he rose with all power in his hands.

When my hope is dashed upon my rock of regret, I call on Jesus and he answers me with a new dream based on my future and not my past. When my hope is dashed upon the rock of missed opportunities and squandered resources, I call on Jesus and he answers me with a new dream based on his resources, which include the cattle on a thousand hills. When my hope is dashed upon the rock of sleep deprivation and too little time, I call on Jesus and he gives me a new dream based on his grace, which is still sufficient for me.

What happens to a dream deferred? Let's not find out.

Maxell inserts poetic verse as the front matter of this sermon. Well-placed, it serves at least two important functions setting the sermonic stage. First, the questions of Hughes's poem signal that a textured and thoughtful response will follow. The leading question, "What happens to a dream deferred?" implies that the message will address personhood as the ground floor of hope upon which dreams begin. Maxell's leading question, like Lettsome's in chapter 1, instigates a searching critique of the oppressive and oppositional social and political forces that diminish human hope. Second, the questions that follow are also substantive, when they point out that dreams are futile if hope is not actualized in time and space; they dry up, stink and rot, and explode.

As Maxell mentions in her opening lines, the poem "A Dream Deferred" invites listeners "to ponder the destiny of an unactualized dream." The preacher takes an imaginative, lateral leap as she strategically emphasizes the role and influence one individual can have within a larger communal struggle. With this established, she, seeking beauty, names the perplexing issues of the communal predicament in inner-city hotspots, and interestingly enough, the city centers she cites are the US cities most impacted by the torrent of southern migrants in the early twentieth century. She poetically avers,

- *Whether the community dries up "like a raisin in the sun" like Detroit,* whose blocks of abandoned homes and businesses speak of the booming automotive industry of times past; or

- *Whether it "festers like a sore and then runs" like Harlem,* whose gleaming, gentrified areas are unable to stave off the bloodletting in its most depressed areas; or

- *Whether it "stinks like rotten meat" like the Pittsburgh neighborhood of Atlanta,* where sex trafficking, drugs, and violent crime run rampant in the shadows of the lights and the family fun of Turner Field; or

- *Whether it "crusts and sugars over" like New York City,* where police brutality still adversely affects the Blacks and the Browns despite their international claims of multiethnic diversity; or

- *Whether it "sags like a heavy load" like the US economy,* that still operates at a suppressed rate for the lower and middle class while the upper class makes billions and gets rewarded with a lower tax rate; or

- *It explodes like the pristine, tree-lined streets of Newtown, Connecticut.* Our experience tells us that a dream deferred is simply no good.

Next, she pivots toward scripture but delays her exposition of the primary text. She quotes instead Proverbs 29, which reads, "Where there is no vision, the people perish." Maxell asks, "Why are communities drying up?" The problems are legion, she suggests, because even in a world filled with visionary leaders, societal problems still mount. A critique of society is followed by an indictment on the church's lack of vision to help persons realize new vistas of opportunity in America. Settling in on a focused critique of church leadership, Maxell turns to the Old Testament record, 1 Samuel 7, that details the relationship between Israel's first king, Saul, and his sole heir, Jonathan. She exposits the passage and sketches the human dilemma of a failed dynastic succession based on bloodline. As Maxell infers, David's unlikely rise to kingship is consequent to Saul's lack of vision to lead his people.

Following her textual probing, the discourse shifts. She begins to tease out an underappreciated aspect of the story. She contends that the text should be interpreted panoramically instead of reading it one-dimensionally. Saul, Jonathan, and his armor-bearer, she describes, had critical roles in securing Israel's defeat of the Philistines. Here the story becomes a teaching lesson on the virtues of collaborative leadership. She says, "We learn that our responsibility as theologians and practitioners of faith requires more than distanced commentary and contemplation in response to God's vision for lives. We are called to be active participants fully engaged in God's work in the world." One of the hermeneutical beauty marks of this sermon rests in its central claim without deference to David. She simply refuses to transport the later conquests of David into the small window of the pericope she considers. Her insights communicate something theologically significant without mentioning David's warrior exploits. The next shift is a call to the listeners of her seminary community to reimagine what corporate concern for community and speaking out entails. When words of justice and hope are spoken to address the multiple crises of community, contends Maxell, innovation is tapped and people are permitted to dream again. The sermon ends in a richly contextualized hopeful crescendo. A dream deferred is not a dream dead. "Just because the dream is deferred," she professes, "doesn't mean that it's dead and since it's not dead there is hope. And that's the good news I bring to you here in this community called Candler this day." Again, she repeats: "Just because the dream has been deferred, doesn't mean that it's dead."

FAITH AND SCIENCE

In recent years considerable theological attention has been devoted to understanding and reconciling views and perspectives on religious practice and scientific exploration. How might the Christian sort out the life he or she lives in the chemistry lab on Monday through Friday with life lived in the prayer closet and on the church pew? In our culture of distrust and cultural fragmentation, how does the preacher paint the homiletical picture before the hearer that respects the internal integrity of both reason and faith? Anti-intellectual sermons continue to abound in many African American congregations today, and this is deeply regretful. We who preach seek to give relevant meaning from premodern correspondences. This is no small task, and has not been since the birth of the European Enlightenment of the seventeenth and eighteenth centuries, also known as the age of reason and science. But how we begin a sermon can make a world of difference to the twenty-first-century enlightened mind.

SERMONIC EXAMPLE ➡

Matthew Riley III[4]
"The New Creation Is in Our Hands"; Revelation 21:4

---

4. Sermon used by permission. Matthew Riley III, a May 2017 alumnus of Howard University School of Divinity, is pursuing further graduate studies in bioethics at Harvard University in Cambridge, Massachusetts. Seminarians' Day of Preaching, a bi-annual event, was birthed in the spring of 2009 to provide graduating master of divinity student preachers a supplemental opportunity to preach a seven-minute sermon in a community-wide chapel service. Of the seven student participants, Mr. Riley preached the closing sermon.

Seminarians' Day of Preaching
Dunbarton Chapel, Howard University School of Divinity
Washington, DC
2017

This excerpt of Matthew Riley III's sermon "The New Creation Is in Our Hands" opens evocatively, urging the listener to ponder the expanse of God's created universe, the beauty of science, and sets the apocalyptic stage for his hearers to live in anticipation of God's plan to renew creation.

Declaiming the consequential effects of humanity's misuse of creation, in adorning cosmology-speak, Riley stokes the sacred imaginations of his divinity school community—neither with the Exodus motif nor the prophetic literature but with apocalyptical imagery pointing to the saving presence of Jesus Christ—who listen attentively as he enters the sermon.

SERMON FRAGMENT: "THE NEW CREATION IS IN OUR HANDS"

In the twenty-first chapter of the book of Revelation, the first through the fourth verses, there are these words.

> Then I saw a new heaven and a new earth; for the first heaven and the first earth had passed away, and the sea was no more. And I saw the holy city, the New Jerusalem, coming down out of heaven from God, prepared as a bride adorned for her husband. And I heard a loud voice from the throne saying: the home of God is among mortals. He will dwell with them; they will be his peoples, and God himself will be with them; he will wipe every tear from their eyes. Death will be no more; mourning and crying and pain will be no more, for the first things have passed away.

This evening, we will consider together the following thought: the new creation is in our hands.

Cosmologists believe that a great deal happened in the first second of time, including the emergence of the four fundamental forces of nature—gravitation, electromagnetism, and the strong and weak nuclear forces. Massive fragments from these early particles increased in temperature, converting hydrogen into helium—and the first stars were born, lighting up the young universe. The material produced by these stars and their supernova explosions produced complex organic molecules that were fundamental to the emergence of life on earth. And in time, life did emerge.

This description of the developing universe that science offers to us—is noteworthy. But somehow the keyword "description" has been confused and conflated with "explanation." Description of the universe has been replaced with explanation for the existence of the universe. And out of this reasoning has come what is perhaps the most widespread and fundamental assumption in the intellectual West today, which is that there is no reality beyond what natural science discovers and that there is no authority or good that is higher than the will of the human person.

Yet, in spite of and notwithstanding these assumptions, the philosophical question of "why is there something rather than nothing?" still remains. The existence of the universe and the laws of nature themselves demand an explanation that stands outside of science.

Nature is not self-explanatory. The physical laws such as gravity and electromagnetism are not self-sustaining or transcendent. The chemical elements such as hydrogen, helium, and carbon are not eternal, but they are bound by time. The laws of nature are not the beginning of all things. And they are not the end. But there is a transcendent reality that dwells outside of space and time. There is truth that stands outside of that which can be observed by science—for we cannot peer through a microscope and investigate the great architect that balanced the earth on its axis.

We cannot experiment on the brilliant engineer that placed the sun and the moon in the sky. We cannot reason with the great lawmaker that conceived and ordained the laws of nature. And we will never be able to understand in our finitude that which is the infinite, self-existent, transcendent entity, which is the ground of our very being.

The emergence of the universe has deep theological meaning, which stems from a long history of theological reflection on a God who is faithful and sustains the world. The great story of our universe is not a story that is separate from God, but it is God's story. It is the story of the creative act of a God who loves us—the first particles, the emergence of stars, the production of elements necessary for human life, the intricacy of the human brain; the soul consciousness that enables us to think and to be—all of this is God's work, brought about by God's hands.

The beauty of *science*—is that it gives us a more robust vision of what God is *like*—science teaches us that God is much bigger—that God is much grander, that God is much-more-awesome, that God is much-*more*-majestic, that God is much more worthy of honor, that God is much more worthy of exaltation, that God is much more worthy of *worship* than perhaps we had previously thought.

When we reflect on the sciences we suddenly become philosophically and theologically overwhelmed by God's love for us. For how could a God so big love us in spite of the small, selfish, and sinful things that we do sometimes? How could a God so glorious love us in spite of ourselves? Like the psalmist cried out—*when* I consider the *heavens*—the works of thy fingers the moon and the stars which thou has ordained, who are we that you are mindful of us oh God? Yes, the sciences teach us a lot about what God is like. But perhaps the sciences also teach us even more about what we humans are like.

For in our text this evening, we receive the promise that new creation is soon to come; and while reflecting on God's promise that new creation is on its way, I could not help but be perplexed by the reality of what we humans did with God's first creation. What we did was exploit it instead of replenish it.

Instead of God, we worshipped money—power—territory—we worshipped big church buildings—we worshipped—heavy offering plates . . . We fell in love with greed, individualism, and selfishness— we embraced poverty, inequality, war, and racism. God gave us the universe, but somehow the cosmos was not good enough—so we abused our power and exploited the poor. We destroyed what God said was good. And as a consequence suffering, pain, sickness, and death came knocking at our doors.

Yes the sciences teach us a whole lot about ourselves. They help us to see clearly that we humans are in need of a second chance after what we did to God's first creation.

And I'm so glad this evening, that somewhere I read that God is a God of a second chance. I'm so glad this evening, that God who is rich in mercy, grace, and love—has a plan for putting creation back right again. And we know that God has a plan.

For when we search the Holy Scriptures over, we find that the Matthean, Markan, Lukan, and Johannine texts are all stories about God putting creation back right again—stories about when Jesus restored the sight of the blind, stories about just a little small touch which healed the woman with the issue of blood. Stories about a new creation where all of God's children are fed. A new creation where the power and transformative vision of heaven comes down and is birthed on earth. This is the new creation that Jesus Christ launched.

—CRAFTING STRATEGY: DELIVERING PROPHETIC MESSAGING IN MELODIC METER—

Hearing music of every genre helps preachers to stay attuned to the affairs of the human heart. Music has the capacity to touch people at the soul level, and thus can become an opening for spiritually resourcing persons who have lost their way. The sociopolitical force of Jesus's revolutionary message challenging oppressive regimes that dehumanize and exploit the poor and needy are parabolic teachings in the Bible that can be read lyrically and melodically to good effect. Similarly, as with parables, hip-hop artists use rhetorical strategies that require decoding.

CST1: LISTEN TO MUSIC ABOUNDING IN VIVID IMAGERY.

SERMONIC EXAMPLE ⇨

Lecrae
"Welcome to America"
Album: *Anomaly*
2014[5]

The deployment of the Exodus preaching paradigm is inferential in Christian rapper Lecrae's trendsetting song "Welcome to America." Refusing Christianese God-talk, Lecrae lifts the veil of America's race predicament and names as sin the exploitive practices of capitalism and the vices it encourages. Lecrae's lyrics chronicle three perspectives on American life. In verse 1, we meet an African American streetwise teen lamenting his station and imagin-

---

5. Lyrics used by musician's permission. See Lecrae's music video "Welcome to America" at https://youtu.be/qlx9jZcBkNA.

ing what his life could have been free of exposures to guns, crack-cocaine, and street hustling.

> Uh I was made in America land of the free, home of the brave
>
> Yea made in America
>
> Momma told me that I belong here
>
> Had to earn our stripes had to learn all rights had to fight for a home here
>
> But I wouldn't know a thing about that
>
> All I know is drugs and rap
>
> I probably could have been some kinda doctor
>
> Instead of holding guns and crack
>
> I was born in the mainland
>
> Great-grandpa from a strange land
>
> He was stripped away and given bricks to lay
>
> I guess you could say he a slave hand
>
> But I was made in America

Lecrae then flexes his knowledge of military history. He contextualizes his rhythmic address. Verse 2 speaks to the nature of personal sacrifice and our nation's disregard of personhood and human dignity. The song recalls the valor and unjust treatment of Black enlisted troops in America's wars who returned from fighting abroad to receive second-class treatment at home.

> Man, I'd die for America
>
> I served my time for America
>
> Got shot, shot back, went to war, got back and ain't nobody give a jack in America
>
> I could've lost my life, boy, I lost my wife
>
> I can't even get right in my homeland
>
> Cold sweats, hold tecs, paranoid looking out for a threat in my own land
>
> I was trained in America

How'd they get up in them planes in America?

Flew them right into the buildings

Taking out civilians

People getting killed in America?

And I'm still in America

Though America ain't feeling me

I went to war for this Country

Turned around came home and you drillin' me?

When y'all free here saying you don't wanna be here

Well, you probably couldn't breathe here

If I didn't load a couple magazines here

Y'all just complain in America

The song's uncomplicated hook "Welcome to America" loops five times between each verse. This reinforces the fact that despite being a nation of many cultures, cultural difference in America is repeatedly viewed through binary lenses—lenses of state-rule and White normativity rather than true democracy where all citizens are accorded dignity and equal respect. In subversive critique, Lecrae couches witty hip-hop sophistry to achieve two primary goals: to unmask deceptive practices that stifle human flourishing in America and around the globe and to remind America's citizens that despite the poor and privileged bifurcation that is America, gratitude for mercy is always in order for an apostate society that has repeatedly taken God's beneficence for granted.

As a voice of conscience, Lecrae ends the track leaving listeners to ponder the social insecurities that accompany immigrants who arrive at America's shores in pursuit of the crops of Canaan. Naming the facts of the immigrant's perception, Lecrae lyricizes:

Got plenty food in your nation

I can tell cause a lot of y'all are overweight

I already work for y'all

106

I'm in the sweatshops making these shirts for
y'all

Now I ain't getting money, go to bed hungry

But I make some exports for y'all . . .

THORNS AND THISTLES: LISTENING CRITICALLY AND HOSPITABLY

Tepid talks might satisfy the catechized believer, but if preachers fail to poetically inject into their sermons *justice-to-hope* themes and reclaim an assertive,
more courageous speech-act posture, an opportunity to reach a generation of
would-be faithful Christian converts in communities on the brink of collapse
will have been forfeited. I am not suggesting that preachers should accommo-
date to culture uncritically and run the risk of having the preacher's peculiar
news of God's freedom in Christ debased or ensnared by the spiritual and
theological relativism of secular society. What I am implying is that preachers
stand to grow in prophetic leadership when they engage in hospitable listening to religiously divergent, yet aesthetically rich rhetorical discourse not suit-
able for the sanctuary.

Hospitable preachers must be fearless scrutinizers of hip-hop culture. These
preachers, with their ears to the ground, are not only in the best position
to engage the psyche of listeners engaging daily life complications in mean
inner-city streets or in cushy suburbia; they, reaching beyond congregational
culture, know that "if prophetic preaching is to be restored to a vibrant place
in the pulpits of America, it will be necessary for [them] to operate with a
twenty-first-century understanding of the message they are being called upon
to declare."[6] Preachers who dare to listen to what the popular culture hears and
speaks best embody what it is to uphold Jesus's commission to move out into
the world with a revolutionary witness (Matt 28), for they have secured a certain kind of moral authority "to call people back from the worship of Baal and
other idols . . . and attach twenty-first-century identities to those false gods."[7]

Preachers should always seek to pair imagination with proclamation, naming
concretely God's vision for addressing, for example, the idolatrous practices
and abuse of power in church and societal sin. Second, the preacher should
also speak to shape consciousness. The good news of Jesus Christ "does something—it names, provokes, encourages, teaches, and inspires faith—on God's

6.   Marvin McMickle, *Where Have All the Prophets Gone? Reclaiming Prophetic Preaching in America* (Cleveland: Pilgrim 2006), 219.

7.   Ibid.

behalf."[8] To broadcast the good news prophetically as humanizing speech, you, the preacher, must actually see your proclamatory assignment as a real persuasive act. Taking time to select the right word or phrase is critical.

Listeners may not remember the minute details of the message, but they will remember a fitly spoken word that's well placed in the sermon. We craft our language, using rhetorical devices, such as irony, repetition, epistrophe, metaphor, amplification, simile, and so on, to help the listener obtain a theological vision of God and humanity at work to advance God's kingdom of God agenda by promoting wellness, encouraging life, fighting for human dignity, and championing freedom for all humankind.

Third, the preacher will want to find the right pitch and establish a rhythm that is authentic and not contrived. Evocative speech does not need to be bombastic declaration; much of what the preacher can accomplish to call people to confront injustice can be handled with a dramatic whisper. Paying attention to listener cues as one unfolds the sermon is critical. Listeners establish buy-in when the preacher is mindful of modulation and tone. It will not matter what the preacher says if what is said lacks clarity. Hand gestures, good eye contact, and attention to timing and delivery aid sermon embodiment. Preachers do well to remember that what we do in the pulpit shapes consciousness. One way to do so un-prophetically is to make your signature style or customary approach an idol god. To lift the tragically ugly to the poetic beautiful, *Exodus preaching makes use of language and culture.*

---

8. Gilbert, *Journey and Promise*, 11.

EXERCISE

Gather a small group of peers together in a small chapel or sanctuary and present a three-to-five-minute presentation, one on manuscript and another without it. Solicit their feedback on your delivery technique. This is not a critique session on the sermon's theological content; your listeners should only focus on what your voice and body are doing in the moment.

Ask them to rate your performance on a scale from 1 to 5 and suggest improvements. On a second pass, revise your introduction to be heard in a different way using both manuscript and no manuscript approaches. Regarding revision and creative wordsmithing, some of the most intriguing prophetic messages start with a run of startling statistics before getting into the meat of the passage or analysis of the situation.

Chapter Six

PREACHING JESUS "OF THE GOSPELS"

Take me to the alley . . .
to the afflicted ones . . . lonely ones
That somehow lost their way.

—Gregory Porter, *Take Me to the Alley*[1]

How does one preach Jesus with eye and ear to his religion and relationship with humanity? Too often preaching separates Jesus from his personhood and the teaching biographies—the Gospels—that speak of his coming, earthly ministry, death, departure, and promised return. Jesus came to serve and save, and both are consequential to a life of faith. To separate the two is to render a gospel having no effect for the afflicted and lonely ones—the "expendables" of the lower strata for whom the Jesus of the Gospels advocates.

And how does one go about sermon preparation from exploration of rhetorical situation to proclamation of the Word of God? I have said elsewhere that the most fundamental task of the preacher is to interpret Scripture within human community, in service to Jesus Christ. This fundamental task is critically important because the preacher who goes to Scripture carries out a sacred duty on the congregation's behalf.[2] She is entrusted by God and community to understand, nurture, and nourish the church's life in critical and constructive ways. To do this he must broaden his homiletical outlook

---

1. Gregory Porter, *Take Me to the Alley: Studio Album* (Blue Note Records, 2016).

2. Kenyatta R. Gilbert, *The Journey and Promise of African American Preaching* (Minneapolis: Fortress, 2011), 7.

and learn how to communicate the gospel effectively as a good and faithful steward of the Word.

The focus of this chapter is to lay out a strategic and practical plan for developing the sermon. Moving the journeying preacher from exploration of situation to the risky task of proclamation, this four tasks sermon plan incorporates a topic proposal, sermon brief, sermon manuscript (with analysis), and post-proclamation questions of sermon critique. There is joy in preaching, but it is a solemn undertaking for sure. While listening to sermons, people are on a spiritual hunt looking to see if their life can be bettered for having heard a preacher whom it is basically assumed has been in the presence of God to receive what God desires the community to know, consider, and perform.

Preaching is fundamentally humanizing speech about justice, recovery, and hope. It has an emancipatory agenda in the sense that it conveys an outlook of divine purpose at particular moments in time for persons in particular settings where biblical, theological, historical, and cultural considerations are principal determiners for how it will be preached and heard. And while God is guarantor and arbiter on what makes religious discourse divinely inspired, and though the gospel we preach needs no improvement or requires no human validation, God nevertheless chooses to use human beings to accomplish God's saving agenda in time and space. What this means in a practical sense is that preachers should be stewards of the Word and faithful to the task of honoring God and the people with their best offerings.

What follows are sermon preparation resources for guiding the preacher's movement from situation, topic, or text to the performed sermon. Much of what is presented is adapted from the *Four Tasks (Trivocal) Sermon Preparation Plan* I first introduced in chapter 4 of my first publication, *The Journey and Promise of African American Preaching*. While the theory and basic framework that undergird the method is essentially unchanged, additional helps and certain modifications have been made to improve readability and promote practical usefulness when crafting sermons specifically about justice and hope.

—CRAFTING STRATEGY: MOVING FROM EXPLORATION TO PROCLAMATION—

In the *Four Tasks Sermon Preparation Plan*, the preacher essentially moves from *Exploration* (gathering and listening) to *Clarification* (shaping and claiming) to *Internalization* (crafting and indwelling) to *Proclamation* (seeing and saying). Before outlining this plan, let us consider the principal marks of African American prophetic preaching (Exodus preaching). Exodus proclamation is emancipatory speech that speaks truth and promise, judgment and restoration, and life and hope. It stands against idolatry, self-serving behavior, and deceptive human practices; it broadcasts hope in contexts of misery and despair; it couples speech performance with ethical action to recover muted voices; and it summons language and art to alter human perception for the purpose of revealing life as it is meant to be.[3]

THORNS AND THISTLES: POOR PLANNING MUDDLES EXECUTION

It bears repeating: no particular preparatory sermon development strategy or mastery of technique ensures that a sermon preached will be prophetic, or for that matter effectual at all. But for the preacher who desires to trumpet a certain sound about justice and hope in an age of dwindled empathy, human tragedy, and social decay, that preacher will know that fitting and faithful preaching requires discipline. There is no way to get around it. What goes into preaching cannot be left up to chance and what gets accomplished in preaching the gospel is of great consequence. Preaching transforms lives. Therefore, discourse fittingly spoken in God's name and on God's behalf insists that the preacher's vocation of speaking life in needed spaces be taken seriously.

Only preachers who are dedicated to preparation profit the worshipping community.

---

3. African American priestly preaching (sacramental preaching) bears its own characteristic marks. Sacramental proclamation is meditational speech that encourages through a variety of emphases and practices the Christian and spiritual formation of hearers; it places great emphasis on moralistic concerns; it focuses on the worship environment and institutional maintenance and preservation; it interprets the requirements of covenantal obligation; and it endeavors to religiously and communally socialize individuals for a life of discipleship. And finally, African American sagely preaching (wisdom preaching) carries its set of key accents. Wisdom proclamation interprets the common life of worshippers and confers upon them wisdom; it daringly speaks in the context of radical social and ecclesial change; it seeks to decode the signs, symbols, and texts of the community of faith; and it bestows biblical wisdom and realistic hope for future generations.

THE FOUR TASKS OF SERMON PREPARATION

1. EXPLORATION

CST 1: ASK, WHAT HAS DRIVEN ME TO THE TASK OF PREPARATION?

The principle objective of the exploration task is to obtaining a clear assessment of what has driven the preacher to the task of sermon preparation? Have matters pertaining to

- Congregational relations
- Worship renewal
- Spiritual growth
- Personal and social sin
- Mission and evangelism
- Social justice
- Personal suffering
- Cultural identity
- Income inequality

presented themselves in such a way that invites the preacher's investigative probing? In addition, mindfulness of the ministry occasion or ministry task in which the preacher will engage such issues is paramount. Although congregants should hear how the message of the gospel addresses dilemmas in church settings, as prophetic discourse, Exodus proclamation cannot and should not be enclosed in the preacher's Sunday morning holy assignment. Whether proclamation goes forth in a chapel service or prison cell or at a prayer breakfast, where two or three gather, the God who stands on the side of justice may choose to show up in the preacher's voice at any moment.

In chapter 4 we discussed the importance of naming reality—giving a name to occurrences and adverse conditions that present a *rhetorical situation* (combination of persons, events, or imperfection marked by urgency) that invites the sermon's address. For the sermon to become consequential the nature of the potential or actual problem must rise to the level of detection. While none wants to hear a litany of problems dumped into a single sermon, sketching out a catalogue of public issue oriented or expressly ecclesial concerns adds homiletical grist to the preacher's work folder when thinking about the gospel as God's incarnational witness for our world.

CST2: COLLABORATIVE BRAINSTORMING WITH ONE'S MINISTRY STAFF AND CLERGY PEERS—OR WITH A CROSS-SECTION OF LAITY, COMMUNITY ACTIVISTS, PHYSICIANS, AND UNCHURCHED PERSONS— COULD BE A FRUITFUL EXERCISE FOR GENERATING SERMON IDEAS.

Holding to the notion that those within the ecclesiastical fold are the subject matter experts who should not be consulted when engaging spiritual or religious concerns closes off the preacher's exploratory field of vision. Of course, entertaining too many voices in a conversation every time a person is scheduled to preach not only can undermine the preacher's authority and diminish the preacher's voice, it may cloud the preacher's spiritual reception and judgment if and when God needs a one-on-one with the preacher.

A *brainstorm* is defined as a spontaneous group discussion to produce ideas and ways of solving problems. *Intergenerational/Cross-sectional Brainstorming* is an exercise of corporate reading, hearing, and sharing of one's initial impressions on a selected passage of Scripture and/or public issue or ecclesial concern, which emphasizes mutually influential collaboration between age groups and intra/extra community representatives.

RULES OF ART

1. Read, meditating on a pre-selected passage.

2. Pose a question or concern the text raises for you.

3. In no more than *three* sentences, share critical insights.

QUESTIONS TO CONSIDER

What do I see in and hear from the text? What does the text say or seem to say? What details stand out?

Scripture Text: Luke 4:17b-21

He [Jesus] unrolled the scroll and found the place where it was written: "The Spirit of the Lord is upon me, because he has anointed me to bring good news to the poor. He has sent me to proclaim release to the captives and recovery of sight to the blind, to let the oppressed go free, to proclaim the year of the Lord's favor."

BASIC INSIGHTS

This is the vision of Jesus and his proclamation in wide scope.

The Good News = Word of God as provision for the poor; freedom for the locked down and locked up; removal of physical and spiritual cataracts.

This text points to the fact that community wellness is of divine concern.

*The *Topical Proposal* mentioned in chapter 4 would be housed here in this Four Tasks Sermon Plan.

2. CLARIFICATION

The second principal task for mapping the sermon is to intensify the exploration and arrive at a claim statement. What will I say based on what I have gathered and heard? What can I expect to hear in light of the world of the text and local, national, and world events? What must be said that only I can say given my probing of the text, issue, or concern? Is God active or seemingly passive in the text under consideration and in the world we presently inhabit? If active, where? If silent, why? Will this be a message of challenge, rebuke, hope, or instruction or some combination? The claim at which you arrive should have an answer or at the very least a thoughtful response to these sorts of questions.

Serious wrestling yields a bounty of exegetical fruit. But clearly all of what is discovered can't and should not make the final cut at the stage of crafting the manuscript. Now before any biblical, theological, or congregational exegesis takes place, take some time for self-critical examination. Since we cannot bracket out ourselves from the texts we interpret ask yourself:

- What am I bringing to the rhetorical situation and biblical passage?
- Can I identify any causes that conflict with my willingness to confront the rhetorical situation or interrogate the text?
- Am I excited? Anxious? Offended? Clear-headed? Angry? Alert?

Take note of any changes in feeling and mood throughout process.

Now it's time to engage the process thinking about drawing on scholarly resources—critical tools—to better acquaint you with the world of the biblical text. Attending critically to the biblical text is to discuss the text's social location, canonicity, textual genre, theological content, and so on. Again, because we bring ourselves to the texts we interpret, it will simply not do to begin or end one's exegetical work without asking the question, *"What does this text mean in relation to who I am as a communally shaped being having a share as co-participant with the God of Scripture who wants me to understand, interpret, and fittingly share the Word to assist the population I serve?"*

*The *Sermon Brief* mentioned in chapter 2 would be housed here in the Four Tasks Sermon Plan.

CST3: SHAPE YOUR CLAIM. ANSWER THREE CLAIM-GENERATING QUESTIONS: WHAT CAN I SAY? WHAT CAN I EXPECT? WHAT MUST I SAY?

In shaping the claim, the preacher's exploratory momentum shifts toward isolating the rhetorical situation and biblical text's findings to state a claim. Time must be set aside for exegetical reflection and conversation with the biblical commentators. After teasing out exegetical finds, the preacher names what is seen.

The preacher inquires:

What am I lamenting? What can I hope for? Where is God? What is God actively doing in the text? Can anything be celebrated in the focus passage? Is there an image, picture, or path pointing toward a just end or hopeful vision in or surrounding the passage?

Claims become discernible following this line of questions.

QUESTION ONE (Q1)—DECLARATION

What can I say? (A declaration *about* the here-and-now in light of our *human predicament*)

Examples:

- We live in a world of pain and grief that unsettles our faith, fuels our fears, and calls us into deep spaces of lament.
- The picture of a good life fades after a loved one dies tragically.

- Love that matters is too little revealed in our times because we are uncaring, impatient, and pushy.

- When good things happen in our lives we rejoice, but our first inclination is to remove God from our lives when we encounter the bad.

QUESTION TWO (Q2)—PROPOSITION

What can I expect? (A proposition *for* the here-and-now in light of *divine intervention*)

Examples:

- When we recognize that our ultimate hope is in Jesus Christ, we find assurance of divine support.

- As we listen to God's voice in times of quiet, we will find our paths clear.

- Since the love of God conquers death, I can bank on love's greatest promise to the believer—eternal life.

- We can be confidently assured that a way will be made in difficult times because God is ever present.

QUESTION THREE (Q3)—APPROPRIATION

What must I say? (A synesthetic appropriation *in* the here-and-now in light of a *sacred promise*)

The preacher offers a "synesthetic" appropriation in the here-and-now in light of a known sacred promise.

In science, *synesthesia* is a neurological phenomenon, which refers to perceptual experience, where a "sense impression" is produced as one sense or part of the body stimulates another sense.

As I think about the term in the homiletical context, it describes the revelatory "aha" (sense impression) that is produced when a preacher's spiritual moorings and theology meet and interact with a preacher's disciplined biblical, historical, theological, and sociocultural study of text and situation.

The idea of promise has to do with the revelation of God, which is dynamic because it takes place in history and is not abstract, but is, as systematic theologian James H. Evans Jr. asserts, "permanent, final, and ultimate in the sense that what we know of God is absolutely trustworthy." "All of Christianity," he rightly claims, "stands or falls with the promise of God to be faithful to God's word."[4]

The preacher who offers God's revelation to the listening congregation understands that her or his role is not that of future or fortune-telling, but the announcement that affirms that "while we may not know what God will do in the future, we do know that God's future acts will not contradict God's past act . . . that [Jesus Christ's] future identity will not contradict his past identity."[5]

Examples:

- We know that with Jesus's power we can overcome the most perplexing circumstances.

- We understand that when the Holy Spirit's power rests on us we are given power to overcome sin and have liberty of conscience.

- We recognize that new life in Christ is ours since we have been redeemed by Christ's sacrificial love.

- We can believe that our future is secure because God is on our side.

EXAMPLE: BASED ON JOHN 11:17-39—THE RAISING OF LAZARUS

Q1—WHAT CAN I SAY? [DECLARATION]

We live in a world of pain and grief that unsettles our faith, fuels our fears, and calls us into spaces of deep lament.

Q2—WHAT CAN I EXPECT? [PROPOSITION]

But when we recognize that our ultimate hope is in Jesus Christ, we find assurance of divine support . . .

Q3—WHAT MUST I SAY? [APPROPRIATION]

knowing that with Jesus's power we can overcome the most perplexing of circumstances.

---

4.   James H. Evans Jr., *We Have Been Believers: An African American Systematic Theology*, 2nd ed., edited and introduced by Stephen G. Ray Jr. (Minneapolis: Fortress, 2012), 15.

5.   Ibid., 16.

Basic Claim: We live in a world of pain and grief that unsettles our faith, fuels our fears, and calls us into spaces of deep lament. But when we recognize that our ultimate hope is in Jesus Christ, we find assurance of divine support knowing that with Jesus's power we can overcome the most perplexing of circumstance.

Simplified Claim: When we recognize that our ultimate hope is in Jesus Christ, we find assurance of divine support in a world of pain and grief.

An effectively crafted claim should be congruent with the witness of the text, no matter if the preacher preaches a topical sermon or expository sermon. Also, an effectively crafted claim statement, as stated, could be directly uploaded into the sermon itself.

Take notice, the Clarification task (the exegetical section and second task), is the lengthiest part of the Four Tasks Sermon Preparation report. Give sufficient time to this task, otherwise tasks three and four will be homiletically deficient.

3. INTERNALIZATION

In task three, Internalization, the preacher moves from biblical, theological, sociocultural, and sociopolitical exegetical reflection and issue clarification to the important step of sermon creation (crafting and indwelling the sermon).

In my experience of teaching this sermon preparation approach, internalization is often given curt treatment. Procrastination is the enemy of every preacher! Poor time management, falling in love with and getting lost in exegesis, receiving the late preaching invitation, attending to family responsibilities, negotiating a crowded schedule, intellectual and physical fatigue, lack of focus, and writer's block are the usual culprits of sermon obstruction. Still, I cannot overstate the importance of carefully and faithfully managing the crafting and indwelling process in a disciplined way. What typically cures me in this regard is the dreadful feeling I have when my sermonic presentation falls flat and no one is moved, including myself.

Sermons are offerings, and sometimes we come up short. This notwithstanding, don't take too much consolation here, for similar to the caregiving expectation you would have when seeing a dentist for a toothache or cardiac surgeon for a heart attack, the people of God expect and deserve your best efforts.

CST4: PAIR EXEGETICAL REVELATIONS WITH THE PREACHER'S SACRED IMAGINATION.

In a practical sense, the preacher will want to:

- Determine the movement: expository-deductive/inductive; narrative; mixed narrative; three-point propositional structure, Proctor's Hegelian dialectical approach, and so on.

- Form an Outline: this mapping does not need to be extensive, just logical.

- Compose: Draft and re-draft to (1) *"get it out"* on paper and *"talk it through"*; (2) *shape and arrange*—writing for the ear instead of the eye is crucial to building and sustaining sermon momentum (I have found this process moves more smoothly if what is done in the exegetical sermon brief is brought together sermonically, so begin sermonizing early); (3) polish and rehearse.

While it is good to talk the sermon aloud along the way, take time to read the entire manuscript. Find a sermon listener or ministry colleague you trust and let them hear the message vocally embodied and give you their feedback. Pastoral preaching (here I make no distinct between it and prophetic preaching since pastoral preaching can be prophetic) tends to demand a slightly different preparation strategy just as extemporaneous preaching requires a particular way of preparing in contrast to taking a full manuscript to the pulpit.

Although there's much conversation and debate around which is better (script or not), for justice-to-hope oriented Exodus preaching, I expect to hear a strong diagnosis and handling of the topic/rhetorical situation, which often means drawing in and interpreting statistical data to reinforce message content. Empirical findings should not be jettisoned or left on the floor because a preacher feels she hasn't preached unless she preaches without paper. Placing too much weight on sermon performance often diminishes the theological content sharing in the preaching event. Generating a certain type of antiphonal feedback or interactive frenzy around the message should not be your goal. Still, no matter how well-stocked the message content, the preacher will do violence to the preaching moment if a dispassionate lecture is given rather than a sermon.

4. PROCLAMATION

This final task is the riskiest part of the process. It is about *making it seen* and *getting it said*. So after completing the exploration, clarification, and internalization tasks, the preacher now gives the vision voice to what has been interpreted, crafted, and indwelled.

Will I abandon the manuscript, be guided by notes/outline, or use a full manuscript? Let your gifts, level of experience, and preaching context help you to discern the best method. Finding the right pitch, establishing a rhythm, offering hopeful symbols through descriptive image, and watching out for listener cues are key in shaping listener consciousness. The preacher should remember that the goal of proclamation is to put the gospel in the best possible light.

Finally, the preacher should take the time to solicit feedback from listeners he or she trusts who will be honest and constructive. Sermon critique is essential for growth. Ask yourself:

Did I abandon my claim? Did I leave out important or unimportant information? What voice seemed leading? Prophetic? Priestly? or Sagely? How did the sermon function? Was it kerygmatic, didactic, exhortative, reflective, or parabolic? Did it evoke call-and-response congregational participation; encourage contemplation; inspire sociopolitical action? How did it play? What am I still hearing? What did the people have to say? What did you hope they would say or not say?

SERMONIC EXAMPLE ➡

Kenyatta R. Gilbert
"How Shall We Live?"; Luke 11:1-13
Duke University Chapel
Duke University
Durham, NC

We now turn our attention to a sermon I have preached based on the incarnational witness of Jesus, titled "How Shall We Live?" For teaching purposes, I will use tag words to point out where and when the four key marks of exodus preaching are evident in the sermon. Because sermons are arrested performances, something is always lost after the moment in which they are delivered, and deeper the divide is when the sermon is set to the written page. The intent in looking at the sermon here is not to say, "Do what I do." Rather, the hope in reproducing and working it up is for it be a useful tool for self-assessing your own offering to God.

Basic Claim: God's gift of real presence to a world bereft of compassion, empathy, and regard for neighbor is the site of God's kingdom at hand. By praying as Jesus instructed his disciples, we find a God who meets our needs and teaches us how to give of ourselves in benevolent and gracious ways.

Simplified Claim: God's gift of real presence is the site of God's kingdom at hand. When we pray as Jesus instructs us, we find a God who meets our needs and teaches us to give of ourselves.

Q1: WHAT CAN I SAY? [DECLARATION]

God's gift of real presence to a world bereft of compassion, empathy, and regard for neighbor is the site of God's kingdom at hand.

Q2: WHAT CAN I EXPECT? [PROPOSITION]

By praying as Jesus instructed his disciples, we find a God who meets our needs and teaches us.

Q3: WHAT MUST I SAY? [APPROPRIATION]

how to give of ourselves in benevolent and gracious ways

SERMON ANALYSIS USING FOUR CHARACTERISTICS OF EXODUS PREACHING PARADIGM

SERMON: "HOW SHALL WE LIVE?"

KEY

Unmasks systemic evil and deceptive human practices by means of moral suasion and subversive rhetoric. **Unmasking**

Remains interminably hopeful when confronted with human tragedy and communal despair. **Hope**

Connects the speech act with just actions as concrete praxis to help people freely participate in naming their reality. *Naming*

Carries an impulse for beauty in its use of language and culture.[6] *Beauty*

SERMON WITH FOUR CHARACTERISTICS ANALYSIS

[Jesus] was praying in a certain place, and after he had finished, one of his disciples said to him, "Lord, teach us to pray, as John also taught his disciples." He said to them, "When you pray, say:

Father, hallowed be your name.

Your kingdom come.

Give us each day our daily bread.

---

6.   See *A Pursued Justice: Black Preaching from the Great Migration to Civil Rights* (Waco, TX: Baylor University Press, 2016) for a more comprehensive treatment of these discourse features.

And forgive us our sins,

for we also forgive everyone indebted to us.

And do not bring us to the time of trial."

And he said to them, "Suppose one of you has a friend, and you go to him at midnight and say to him, 'Friend, lend me three loaves of bread; for a friend of mine has arrived, and I have nothing to set before him.' And he answers from within, 'Do not bother me; the door has already been locked, and my children are with me in bed; I cannot get up and give you anything.' I tell you, even though he will not get up and give him anything because he is his friend, at least because of his persistence he will get up and give him whatever he needs.

"So I say to you, Ask, and it will be given you, search, and you will find; knock, and the door will be opened for you. For everyone who asks receives, and everyone who searches finds, and for everyone who knocks, the door will be opened."

It was Holy Week and nearing the close of our academic semester. My grades were soon to be due. And as usual, procrastination had gotten the best of me. I was at my computer, intent on grading assignments. But was quickly drawn away from the task with a click of the mouse. A Good Friday service was being broadcast from Chicago's Trinity United Church of Christ. Prominent preachers, young and veteran, were in the lineup to present sermons based on the seven last sayings of Christ. It must have been one-third of the way into the service when I tuned in. All I knew was that I was going to settle in and watch these dynamic preachers. And then, my ten-year-old daughter walked into the room to teach me one of the greatest lessons a father can learn. That lesson was that a father must not only be physically present for his children, he must be "really" present. That evening, Olivia asked me one of the most penetrating questions she has ever asked. "Daddy, why do you say 'um hum' when you are not listening?" And then, she vanished to her room.

MIT professor Sherry Turkle paints a rather sobering picture of where we as humans are at this time in history. In her book *Alone Together*, she argues that in an effort to customize our lives, we, to the detriment of our families, vocations, personal and communal selves, sacrifice real conversation for connection. "We are constantly communicating," she writes, "and yet not making good connections." **Unmasking**[7]

Because we are always on, too accessible, tied to our iPhones, constantly checking e-mails, our growing network of Facebook friends, or being voyeurs of trending Twitter feeds, we have come to expect more from technology and less from each other. And because our technological devices provide us the illusion of companionship without the demands of friendship, we are prone to sacrifice real presence for pretend empathy. **Unmasking/*Beauty*[8]** She claims that, and I think she is right, our technological devices not only change what we do, they change who we are. Given this sobering assessment, we must ask ourselves, "How shall we live?"

In this eleventh chapter of Luke, the author presents the reader a Jesus who is neither tenderhearted nor patient. Clearly keyed into the community's concerns for daily bread, forgiveness of sins, debt relief, and deliverance from evil forces, Luke's Jesus is a prayer teacher, a sage if you will, schooling his openhearted followers on the basics of spiritual preparation and the devotional life. ***Beauty*[9]**

In response to the disciples' request for spiritual guidance, what is offered to them is Christianity's best-known invocation—"The Lord's Prayer." In fact, this prayer for them is the only prayer that Jesus gives us. It is the model. In its words of petition, we get a glimpse of an alternative reality, what it means to participate with God in repairing the severed lines of communication between creature and creator. As priestly sage, with this prayer, Jesus provides them wisdom for finding safe haven in an unsafe world. ***Beauty*[10]** Luke's Jesus is a prayer teacher. The rabbi of all rabbis. ***Beauty*[11]** The messiah who has come to usher in the kingdom of God. Gathering his followers, performing miracles, preaching the good news to the poor, and

---

7. technological idolatry-deceptive practices

8. "presence for pretend empathy"; self-serving behavior

9. teacher imagery . . . prayer teacher . . . schooling followers

10. word play

11. hyperbolic; teacher imagery

teaching his hearing, yet slow-to-understand followers, the ABCs of prayer and discipleship. *Beauty*[12]

As Luke records it, it is John's example that prompts the disciples' request for Jesus to teach them how to pray. And though the Gospels don't provide us a clear window into John's prayer life, we may assume that during John's wilderness preparation prayer did indeed furnish his ministry. The curious thing to notice about this prayer is that it is exclusively petitionary. Luke's record contains no adoration, thanksgiving, or confession, which suggests that Matthew's liturgically useful version was not its original form. Whatever the case, what we have here in Luke's record are five requests for God to act.

Every petition in the Lord's prayer is a request for nearness: teach us to pray so we can know we are not alone in this world, give us food daily for our bodies, hug us so we might know we have been forgiven, and let your kingdom come, let it come as near as it is out of our reach. These are all requests for real presence, except the final petition: let no trial come our way. Do not bring us into the time of trial.

There is something else to notice here. What we know is that the Lord's Prayer is a prayer about personhood being supported by parenthood. **Naming**[13] Here, in this prayer God is addressed as Father, whose name is to be hallowed. And this is no small thing. This is not an "I" prayer, but a "We" prayer, because in that one word, *Father*, all discrimination, oppression, exploitation, and racism stand condemned.[14] **Unmasking**/**Hope**/**Naming**/*Beauty*[15]

Jesus's disciples are encouraged to pray with the same familiarity with which Jesus prayed. In other words, Jesus says, "Pray like I pray and even the most dim-witted can't get it wrong." *Beauty*[16] To pray in the way Jesus instructs us to pray, is to ready ourselves to move at the breath of God.

---

12. extension of teacher imagery

13. reality of God's care for dignity and worth of all persons irrespective of life station

14. Leonardo Boff

15. All marks present—criticism/hope

16. injection of humor; contemporized speech—not to be taken literally as Jesus's saying

I know many today have a problem with the metaphor "Father." For some, it conjures up memories they'd care not to revisit. **Naming**[17] Come to think of it, even I, over the years, have shifted the language of my address to God . . . instead of beginning with the politically problematic metaphor "Father," I typically begin my public prayers with the phrase "Eternal God." I'm not exactly sure why I do this. Does it have anything to do with my own biological father's untimely death and the abandonment issues that followed? Or, do I do this to rescue myself from the inclusive-language, God-gendering politics surrounding the metaphor? Or, perhaps I choose not to fight the God-wording war because of what I already know to be true . . . and that is, God has always been active and present in my life, even when I've failed to notice. **Unmasking/*Naming*/*Beauty*[18]**

Time and time again, the God we call Father God, Mother God, Heavenly Parent, Creator, or the Man Upstairs, has come to my aid. Time and time again, this God, incarnated as sagely prayer teacher in our text this morning, has taught me, fed me, forgiven me, reigned over my existence, and has delivered me from fear, death, and evil. **Unmasking/Hope**[19] If this prayer teaches us anything, it teaches us that our personhood is supported by God's parenthood. ***Naming*/*Beauty*[20]** So, even when the metaphor breaks down, never does God's love and grace.

I teach homiletics at a historically Black, university-based theological institution in our nation's capital. Each semester I give a tone-setting talk to students who file into my introductory preaching course. Some come with modest concern for preaching, most of them come with "how-to" expectations, on the hunt for tips to cram into their homiletical toolboxes. ***Beauty*[21]** Still others are present with hopes of conquering their fright of public speaking and simply to complete the course with a good grade to show for their efforts.

For good or bad, accompanying the student is always the "stuff" of their lives—personal baggage, narrow theological views, preju-

---

17. human problem with which many can identify; empathetic imagination at work

18. Directly addresses theological chasm of perspective between Christian groups; though significant, God-language wars potentially lead to self-serving behavior and self-deception.

19. naming war bypasses the central message of relationship and divine concern

20. dignity and worth declaration

21. figurative speech

dices, and long-cherished assumptions about what makes for good preaching.

But this year was a little different. What set the tone this year was the presence of a gentleman sitting in silence, listening on intently, with his oxygen tank stationed on the floor at his side and nasal cannula affixed to his nostrils. ***Beauty***[22] He set the tone. For his presence declared to each of us that "you can't preach a gospel you don't believe and can't preach a gospel you are not committed to . . . and you can't preach to those for whom you have no compassion." **Unmasking/*Naming*/*Beauty***[23]

A few weeks into the semester I received an e-mail that was sent to all of this gentleman's professors informing them that he had checked into the hospital, and to please make provisions for him to make up any missed assignments.

I knew nothing about his medical history. I hardly knew him. I knew nothing about the disease that infirmed him. I had no idea how sick he was at the time. What I did know was that he had started seminary five years ago . . . but now, again, his studies were being disrupted. I received a call from him shortly after he was admitted, and this is what he said: "I want to get this preaching thing down . . . I know I am called by God, I want to be a good preacher. I hate to miss your class, but I promise I will read and stay caught up."

I walked into his hospital room and there he lay, barely able to talk. Looking weak and fragile, pausing to catch his breath after each word spoken. I soon noticed that at the foot of his bed were all of the textbooks required for my class. This struck me. The gospel was being preached with his life, and that forceful proclamation was without words. He was committed to staying on task. Here's a man not afraid to die lying before me, but rather more afraid that he would be unable to return to school ***Naming***[24] to give his first sermon. He didn't want to miss his opportunity because of this setback. He wanted to make sure he got the mechanics down. He had no clue that he was preaching . . . no clue that he was preaching the gospel with his life. Of the fifteen enrollees in the course, only one of his classmates went to visit him.

---

22. vivid imagery; flashback; intended to place hearer in the classroom

23. compassion and commitment justice critique; first person pronoun declarative; "presence declared . . . you can't preach" with a commitment to the gospel or without compassion

24. recounting scene honors situation and gives voice to suffering student's reality

These are they who filed into my class the first day, on the hunt for sermon tips, there to conquer their fright of public speaking . . . and yet missing their opportunity to see and experience the gospel before their very eyes . . . training for ministry, and yet missing the gospel. **Unmasking**[25]

Watch him carefully. That was the message from God for me. Watch him carefully. Sitting there with a stigma he cannot shake. *Beauty*[26] A setback that he can manage at best, but that ultimately will not be overcome. An unshakeable condition, kept at bay, **Naming**/*Beauty*[27] because he has been disciplined . . . never resisting treatment, has had a strong faith . . . a meaningful prayer life, and people who care about him.

Watch him, he will teach you how to teach your students. He will teach all of you how to love, and to use the words of Anne Lamont, "to live as if you are dying." He is here to teach you how to live as if you are dying so that you might have a chance to experience some real presence. **Hope**[28]

Friends, "how are we to live?" you ask. I will tell you. We are to live our lives in pursuit of real presence. *Beauty*[29] Giving reverence to God, honoring God's name as holy.

How shall we live? Beauty[30] We shall live praying for God's kingdom to come, not as a far-off illusion but as an ever-coming reality,[31] finding the will to forgive others, as we ourselves require it. We shall live our lives drawn into the presence of a God who is beyond us, not us, unharnessed by our manipulations and Machiavellian schemes . . . live finding that in spite of God being beyond, other, and absolutely free, that this God, to whom Jesus instructs us to pray, is a God who is unafraid to be in relationship with us. In fact, because God is beyond, other, and free . . . God alone has the capacity to be truly

---

25. distracted, self-interested, dim-witted students just as Jesus's disciples were . . . missing opportunity to see kingdom work at hand

26. vivid description

27. hyperbolic

28. dying student is embodiment of hope

29. interactive rhetoric; query sets up a dialogic dynamic sequence—question and response; quick sermon summary

30. rhythm; repetition-building momentum; reinforcement

31. Charles Slattery, *How to Pray : A Study of the Lord's Prayer* (New York: The Macmillan Company, 1920).

intimate with us without disruption or reluctance. God is unafraid to be close . . . even in a society that instructs us to keep our distance from that which comes into our space. **Unmasking/*Naming*/ Hope/*Beauty*** [32]

How shall we live? We shall live by living the Lord's Prayer, refusing to say it, if we aren't willing to live out its reality. Live it, entering God's mystery, and petitioning God for guidance when we can't see our way or have lost our way.

How shall we live? We shall live in human fellowship, remembering that God is father of all. God is father of all or father of none. And to be connected to God is to shun being selfish with others. The daily bread that we pray for is not "mine" but "ours," and the proper and just distribution of daily bread means that the wealthiest one percent get what they need . . . the middle class get what they need . . . and more importantly, those on the lowest wrung get what they need. ***Naming*** [33]

How shall we live? We shall live delivered and set free from whatever holds us prisoners to fate. For freedom is God's gift, and likewise joy. God is the only one who is absolutely free and has the power to work wonders in the world. *How shall we live?* In complete expectancy and hope, in spite of our deathly reality, broken systems, anxieties about our life and those under our care.

How shall we live? Soberly. Recognizing that walking with God companioned by the only prayer that Jesus gives us is to experience real presence in a land of competing claims about what justice looks like, what mercy entails, who is qualified or disqualified to receive human dignity. Whether we are talking about Sabrina Fulton and Tracy Martin's son, Luke and Gail's Zachery, or the royal boy of the Duke and Duchess of Cambridge, or the Black and Brown youth dying in inner-city Chicago, what is common among all is that each one needs and deserves real presence, human dignity, and the security they give. **Unmasking/*Naming*/Hope/*Beauty*** [34]

The Lord's Prayer is not some perfunctory prayer for the faint at heart. This is, at bottom, the gospel. Dr. Martin Luther King Jr.'s mother

---

32. Question all four marks raise: Who is God and why can one rely on God? Proclamatory address—the Good News.

33. proclamation and justice critique

34. declaration

was slain in her church by a mentally deranged person while playing the Lord's Prayer set to song, on the church's piano. *Beauty*[35] No, this is not some shallow prayer. If we carefully consider it, we discover our needs, we discover who is capable of meeting them, we discover that persistence—asking, seeking, knocking—gets rewarded with the gift of divine compassion. One message in the parable that follows the Lord's Prayer is this: if we don't give up, mercy meets us just as grace marches on ahead of us. *How shall we live?* By prayer. Hoping that our blighted horizon will open for each of us newfound opportunities to be. To love. To share. To receive our inheritance from the hands of a gracious parent who loves to give good gifts to those who ask. **Hope/*Beauty*[36]**

I guess I've tried to say too much . . . perhaps you hold the opinion that I've said too little. All I've tried to say is that God's gift of real presence in a world short on compassion, empathy, and regard for neighbor, invites our participation to pray and live into the prayer that Jesus taught his disciples. It is in this prayer that we discover the site of God's kingdom at hand. *How shall we live?* We'll live in pursuit of real presence.

He sat quietly, with his oxygen tank at his side, with a nasal cannula in his nostrils, pen in hand taking notes, contented to hear my tone-setting talk that opening day. Then God's inaudible message spoke to me saying, "Watch him carefully . . . he will set the tone . . . he is not just here to learn how to craft sermons . . . he's here bearing a gift . . . he is the sermon **Hope/*Beauty*[37]** . . . he has come to teach you and your students how to live as if you are dying so that all who have gathered might have an opportunity to experience some real presence.

---

35.   vivid description

36.   proclamation pointing back to the scriptural passage (verses succeeding the prayer)

37.   phrasing; metaphor

➡ E X E R C I S E 1 ⬅

1. Take a moment to catalogue issues that militate against human flourishing and oppose God's agenda of justice and hope. Your list might include:

- Racial bigotry and xenophobia
- Poverty at home and abroad
- Intimate partner violence
- Educational and socioeconomic disparity
- Corporate greed and political malfeasance
- Gender discrimination
- Gun violence and police brutality
- Mass incarceration and prison expansion
- Unchecked materialism
- Gentrification and displacement of the poor
- Sexual trafficking and child molestation
- Environmental neglect and ruination

2. Type each catalogued public issue or topic into the Google search engine. Read three research-based articles on the issue and write down five hard facts. Seek to understand the issue's importance on local, national, and global levels. Framing the issue around specific events or circumstances, especially at the local level, engenders personal concern and increases listener identification.

➡ E X E R C I S E 2 ⬅

Form an intergenerational/cross-sectional homiletical brainstorming session and meet monthly, quarterly, or annually.

➤ EXERCISE 3 ⬅

Review three previously preached sermons and see if you can derive from them a basic claim. After you have discerned a claim, test the sermonic claim and see if it coheres with the sermon's content when you read it again. Edit the manuscript looking for extraneous content not germane to the sermon.

With the same sermons, see if you can detect any of the four marks of the Exodus paradigm. Highlight them in the manner in which I have above. Ask yourself, which mark(s) are most prevalent? Look for ways to sharpen the sermon and polish the script.

Exodus preaching is God speech—holy correspondence for dark times. It dares to name a God on the move who acts lovingly, justly, and righteously. It is good news for the captives who sit in darkness—justice talk called forth from the deep wells of divine wisdom and heard in the wearied throats of people unwilling to bow down to the gods of the ages—a people purposed to revitalize their communities and repair its best legacies in order for their lives to *matter*. It names the Exodus saga, the evocative cries of the Hebrew prophets, and the messianic witness of Jesus Christ hope.

9 781501 832574